Practice Tests Plus

A2 Key also suitable *for Schools*

NEW EDITION

Kathryn Alevizos • Sharon Ashton • Joanna Kosta
with Rose Aravanis

Pearson Education Limited
KAO Two,
KAO Park,
Harlow,
Essex.
CM17 9SR
and Associated Companies throughout the world

www.english.com/practicetestsplus

© Pearson Education Limited 2019

The right of Kathryn Alevizos, Sharon Ashton and Joanna Kosta to be identified as authors of this Work has been asserted by them in accordance with the Copyright, Designs and Patents Act 1988.

All rights reserved. No part of this publication may be reproduced, stored in a retrieval system, or transmitted in any form or by any means, electronic, mechanical, photocopying, recording or otherwise, without the prior written permission of the copyright holders.

First published 2019
Tenth impression 2026
ISBN 978-1-292-27145-3
Set in Helvetica Neue LT 10/12pt and Gill Sans 10/12pt
Printed in Slovakia by Neografia

We are grateful to the following for permission to reproduce copyright material:

Illustration Acknowledgements
John Batten (Beehive Illustration Ltd) 25, 31, 55, 56, 73, 74, 91, 92, 109, 110, 111, 127, 129, 162, 166, 167, 168, 169; **Nigel Dobbyn** (Beehive Illustration Ltd) 30, 31, 56, 57, 74, 75, 92, 93, 111, 128, 129, 165; **Sue Woollatt** (Graham-Cameron Illustration) 164.

Photo Acknowledgements
The publisher would like to thank the following for their kind permission to reproduce their photographs:
123RF.com: Ariwasabi 121, Elenathewise 85, IKO 121, Jim Pruitt 121, leungchopan 85, Olegdudko 14, Rmarmion 122; **Alamy Stock Photo:** Hero Images Inc. 49, 68, Silvia Gerbino 19; **Pearson Education Ltd:** 40, 41, Gareth Boden 67, 85, 103, Jon Barlow 103, Studio 8 104; **Shutterstock.com:** AJR_photo 14, ESB Basic 103, Hugo Felix 14, 67, Kar Tr 50, Morganka 86, Ninikas 16, Robert Kneschke 67, Steffen Bollmann 88
All other images © Pearson Education

PRACTICE TESTS PLUS NEW EDITION RESOURCES

Where to find and how to use

Access on the **Pearson English Portal**:

	Resource	Description	When to use
AUDIO	Test 1 Training activities Tests 1–6	Audio files for Listening tests and Training.	Throughout the book.
	Audioscripts	Full scripts for the Training activities and Tests 1–6.	During or after completing any of the activities or tests as extra support.
WRITING	Sample answers	Three sample student answers for each piece of writing: – email – article – story	When Test 1 training is complete, use with Test 2 Writing. Sample student answers are written using Test 2 questions, the worksheets aim to help students write good answers to these questions.
	Examiner feedback for each sample answer	Examiner feedback on the three sample student answers for each piece of writing: – email – article – story	
	Student activity worksheet by writing genre	Worksheet 1 – email Worksheet 2 – article Worksheet 3 – story Page 1 – focuses on sample answers and examiner feedback on these to help students understand what makes a 'good' answer. Page 2 – builds process writing skills and gives additional language input.	
SPEAKING	Videos	Speaking test About the exam Candidate feedback Frequently asked questions Examiner feedback	Watch with or without the worksheets described below.
	Student activity Worksheets	Worksheet 1 – focus on test format Worksheet 2 – focus on Part 1 Worksheet 3 – focus on Part 2 Worksheet 4 – consolidation Page 1 – focuses on real students' answers and what makes a good response. Page 2 – focuses on building confidence and useful language for the test.	Worksheet 1 – use with *About the exam* video Worksheet 2 – use with *Speaking test video Part 1* Worksheet 3 – use with *Speaking test video Part 2* Worksheet 4 – use alone
	Video transcripts	Speaking test About the exam Candidates' feedback Frequently asked questions Examiner feedback	During or after watching any of the videos as extra support.
VOCABULARY MAPS	Vocabulary maps for over 20 topics	Vocabulary items organised by topic to help students extend their vocabulary.	Find the matching topic and use with any test to build vocabulary.

Access on the **Pearson English App**:

	Resource	Description	When to use
AUDIO	Test 1 Training activities Tests 1–6	Audio files for Listening tests and Training activities.	Throughout the book.
SPEAKING	Videos	Speaking test About the exam Candidate feedback Frequently asked questions Examiner feedback	Watch with or without the speaking test worksheets.
VOCABULARY BUILDING PRACTICE	Topic-based vocabulary practice	Each topic includes a practice exercise on meaning and one on use.	Find the matching topic and use with any test to build vocabulary.

EXAM OVERVIEW

Both the **Cambridge Key English Test** and the **Cambridge Key English Test for Schools**, also known as **KEY** and **KEYfS**, are made up of **three papers**, each testing different abilities in English. The Reading and Writing paper carries 50% of the marks, while the Listening and Speaking papers each carry 25% of the marks. There are three pass grades: A, B and C. Candidates also receive a numerical score on the Cambridge Scale for each of the four skills.

Reading and Writing 60 minutes
Listening 30 minutes (approximately)
Speaking 8–10 minutes (approximately) for each pair of students.

Paper	Format	Task Focus
Reading and Writing 7 tasks, 32 questions	Part 1: Multiple choice 6 short texts, 6 questions, 3 options.	Understanding short messages of different types.
	Part 2: Multiple matching 3 short texts, 7 questions, 3 options.	Read short texts for specific information and detailed comprehension.
	Part 3: Multiple choice long text, 5 questions, 3 options.	Read one longer text for detailed understanding and main ideas.
	Part 4: Gapped text, choose correct words, 6 gaps, 3 options.	Read a longer text and choose missing words to complete it (vocabulary).
	Part 5: Gap fill text, write correct words, 6 gaps.	Read a text and write missing words to complete it.
	Part 6: Write a short email in response to information given (about 25–35 words).	Focus on writing a short message including key information and using appropriate language.
	Part 7: Write a short story based on three pictures, (35 words or more).	Focus on writing a short creative text including key information.
Listening 4 tasks, 25 questions	Part 1: Multiple choice, 5 short recordings, 3 picture options.	Listening for specific information.
	Part 2: Gap fill, short text, 5 gaps.	Listening for specific information. Write missing information in a short text about the recording.
	Part 3: Multiple choice, long recording, 5 questions, 3 options.	Listening for specific information, feelings and opinions.
	Part 4: Multiple choice, 5 short recordings, 5 questions, 3 options.	Listening for the main idea or message.
	Part 5: Matching, long text, 5 questions, 8 options.	Listening for specific information.
Speaking 4 tasks	Part 1: Introductory phase, examiner-led conversation.	Candidates give personal, factual information and answer questions about their daily life, interests, likes, etc.
	Part 2: Collaborative task. Visual prompts.	Candidates compare, describe and express opinions based on picture prompts. Follow-up discussion led by examiner on the same topic.

CONTENTS

Practice Test 1 **with Training activities**	**6**
Reading and Writing	6
Listening	26
Speaking	40
Practice Test 2 **with Tip strips**	**46**
Reading and Writing	46
Listening	56
Speaking	62
Practice Test 3	**64**
Reading and Writing	64
Listening	74
Speaking	80
Practice Test 4	**82**
Reading and Writing	82
Listening	92
Speaking	98
Practice Test 5	**100**
Reading and Writing	100
Listening	110
Speaking	116
Practice Test 6	**118**
Reading and Writing	118
Listening	128
Speaking	134
Grammar bank	**136**
Speaking bank	**156**
Writing bank	**160**

Visuals for Speaking tests	**164**
Test 1	164
Test 2	165
Test 3	166
Test 4	167
Test 5	168
Test 6	169
General questions	**170**

OVERVIEW
PAPER 1: READING AND WRITING

About the paper

The Reading and Writing paper lasts 60 minutes and there are seven parts. Parts 1–5 are reading tasks. Parts 6–7 are writing tasks.

- In Reading and Writing Parts 1–3, you are given a variety of reading texts. You answer different types of questions to show that you can understand the main message and some of the details of the texts.
- In Reading and Writing Parts 4 and 5, you are given texts with gaps for you to complete. You must show that you can use language correctly by finding the missing words.
- Reading and Writing Parts 6 and 7 are both guided writing tasks.

Reading Parts 1–3

Part 1
In Part 1, you read six short texts. These will include emails, signs, notices, text messages, labels and adverts. There is one multiple-choice question for each text. You have to choose from three options the answer which is closest to the overall meaning of the text.

Part 2
In Part 2, you read a simplified newspaper, internet or magazine article. The article will contain three short texts. The texts are all on the same topic and contain similar ideas and information. The texts can be about people, places or events. There are seven questions and you have to match each one with the correct text. This part of the paper tests your ability to find specific information by reading quickly.

Part 3
In Part 3, you read a simplified newspaper, internet or magazine article. This time there is one long text. You have to answer five three-option multiple-choice questions about the text to show that you can understand the main ideas and some of the details of a longer text. You may also have to answer questions on the opinions and feelings of the writer.

Reading Parts 4 and 5

Part 4
In Part 4, you read a simplified, factual article. This may come from a newspaper, magazine, the internet, or an encyclopedia. The text contains six gaps and for each one, you need to choose the right word from **A**, **B** or **C** to complete the text. These words will usually be verbs, nouns, adjectives and adverbs. This part of the paper tests your ability to read a text and use vocabulary correctly.

Part 5
In Part 5, you read one or two short emails or messages. There are six gaps and you have to think of the right word to complete each one. There is an example at the beginning (0). The missing words will be grammar words such as auxiliary verbs, prepositions, determiners and pronouns. You must spell the words correctly. This part of the paper tests your understanding and knowledge of grammar and text structure.

Writing Parts 6 and 7

You must do two pieces of writing.

- The first is a short message, usually an **email** (Part 6). You write 25 words or more for this part.
- The second is a **story** (Part 7). You look at three pictures and write the story shown in the pictures. You write 35 words or more for this part.

You should spend about 20 minutes on the writing tasks. That includes the time to think before you start writing and the time to check what you have written.

You get the same number of marks in Part 6 and in Part 7 (15 marks each), so you must try to do both well.

Examiners use a mark scheme to decide which band your answer falls in. There are five bands, from 0 to 5. Band 5 is the best. To get a band 5:

- you must include all the information needed (all three points in Part 6 and all three pictures in Part 7)
- your writing must be clear and easy to understand, with good spelling and punctuation
- you must organise your writing in a way that helps the reader understand your meaning.

Your answer does not have to be perfect to get a band 5. However, you can go down one or more bands if your writing is hard to understand, if you don't write enough or if you miss out any of the important information needed.

Part 6

In Part 6, you are given a short text (a note, an email or a postcard from a friend) or some instructions. These tell you what you need to write. There are always three pieces of information that you must include in your email or note. This part of the paper tests your ability to communicate a message to a friend in writing.

Part 7

In Part 7, you write a story. You are given three pictures. Your task is to write the story shown in the pictures. You must include information from all three pictures in your story. You should describe what you see in the pictures and link the events together using simple connecting words such as 'if', 'and', 'so', 'because', etc. This part tests your ability to write a short narrative.

See WRITING BANK for sample answers, useful language and practice

See GRAMMAR BANK for reference and practice

PART 1: TRAINING

Focus on the instructions

1   Look at the exam task on page 9 and 11.
    a   How many questions do you have to answer?
    b   How many options do you have to choose from for each question?

Focus on the questions

1   Look at question **1** on page 9. What kind of text is this?
    a   an email
    b   a text message
    c   a notice

2   Where might you see it? Underline the words that help you decide.
    a   in a theatre
    b   in a school
    c   in a music shop

3   The answer to question **1** on page 9 is **B**. Underline the words in the notice that match the meaning of **B**.

4   Why are **A** and **C** wrong? What is Mr Jones telling students to do in the notice?

5   Now look at question **2**. What kind of text is this?
    a   an email
    b   a notice
    c   a message posted on the internet

6   Now answer these questions about question **2**.
    a   Who wrote the message? Who do you think she is writing to?
    b   What is her problem? Underline the words that tell you.
    c   Read the question and the message. What is Hannah doing? Is she asking for information, or giving information? How do you know?
    d   Read options **A**, **B** and **C**. Which one matches Hannah's reason for writing this message?

7   Look at question **3**. What kind of text is this?
    a   an email
    b   a sign
    c   a text message

8   Look at question **3** again and answer these questions.
    a   Where would you see it?
    b   Who can use this equipment?
    c   Is it OK to use the equipment when it is raining?
    d   Read the three options **A**, **B** and **C**. Which one says the same thing as the sign?

PART 1: TRAINING READING AND WRITING

Part 1

Questions 1 – 6

For each question, choose the correct answer.

1

> Quiet please!
> Students are using this room to practise for the end-of-term concert.
> Mr Jones

- A Mr Jones would like students to practise quietly.
- B Mr Jones does not want people to talk loudly here.
- C Mr Jones wants to know which students were noisy.

2

> Hi everyone,
> I've lost my phone so don't try to call or text me! However, I'll be near my computer most of the day.
> Hannah

Why did Hannah write this message?

- A to tell her friends how to contact her
- B to find out if anyone has seen her phone
- C to check if her friends are going out today

3

> **Highlands Park**
> Outdoor fitness equipment for over 12s only
> *Danger* – don't use in rain

- A You should not exercise here in wet weather.
- B It's not safe to use this equipment at the moment.
- C Children under 12 must be with an adult when using this equipment.

Part 1: Training

9   Look at question 4 on page 11. What kind of text is this?
    a   an email
    b   a notice
    c   a text message

10 Now answer these questions about question 4.
    a   Who are Pete and Jenny – friends or brother and sister? How do you know?
    b   Underline the verbs in options **A**, **B** and **C**. What is the difference between *lend* and *borrow*? What does *return* mean?
    c   Read the message carefully. Decide which option is the answer. Why are the other two wrong?

11 Look at question 5. What kind of text is this?
    a   an email
    b   a sign
    c   a text message

12 Now answer these questions about question 5.
    a   Where might you see it?
    b   Read option **A**. Is the sign giving information about opening hours?
    c   Read option **B**. Does the sale begin or end on May 18th?
    d   Read option **C**. What is happening on May 18th?
    e   Decide which option means the same thing as the sign.

13 Look at question 6. What kind of text is this?
    a   an email
    b   a notice
    c   a message posted on the internet

14 Look at question 6 again and answer these questions about it.
    a   Who wrote the message? Who do you think she is? Who do you think Harry is?
    b   Read option **A**. Has Harry already started his painting?
    c   Read option **B**. Does she say anything about helping him?
    d   Read option **C**. Is she asking when Harry will finish his painting?
    e   Choose **A**, **B** or **C** and underline the words that helped you choose.

4

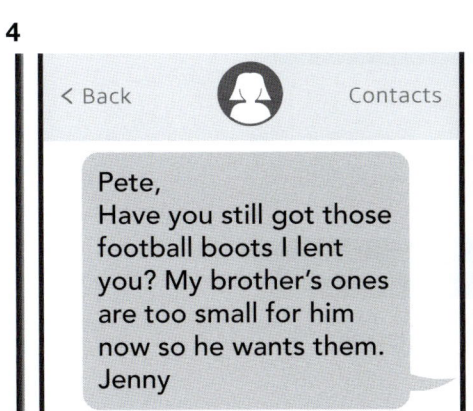

Jenny is asking Pete to

A lend her some football boots.

B return some football boots to her.

C borrow some boots from his brother.

5

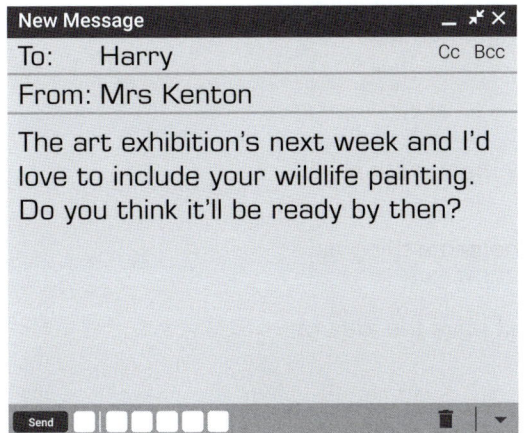

A Opening hours will change on May 18th.

B A big clothes sale begins here on May 18th.

C It won't be possible to shop here after May 18th.

6

> **New Message**
> To: Harry
> From: Mrs Kenton
>
> The art exhibition's next week and I'd love to include your wildlife painting. Do you think it'll be ready by then?

What is Mrs Kenton doing in this email?

A suggesting a subject for Harry's painting

B offering to help Harry with his painting

C checking how soon Harry can finish his painting

PART 2: TRAINING

Focus on the instructions

1   Look at the exam task on page 13.
    a   How many questions do you have to answer?
    b   How many options do you have to choose from for each question?

Focus on the questions

1   Look at the questions and the title of the article on pages 13 and 14. Answer the questions.
    a   What is the article about?
    b   How many questions are there?
    c   How do you answer each question?

2   Read the article quickly. What are three people doing? Tick (✓) the correct phrase.
    • Describing their favourite museum
    • Saying how they feel about museums
    • Telling people to go to museums more often
    • Suggesting some good museums to go to

3   Look at question **7**. Read it carefully and answer the questions.
    a   Read all the texts quickly. Underline anything the people say that you think is about the idea of 'travel'.
    b   Read your underlined parts again. Which of the texts says the same thing as question **7** but in different words?

4   Now look at question **8**. Read it carefully and answer the questions.
    a   Read all the texts quickly. Underline anything the people say that you think is about the idea of visiting a museum several times.
    b   Read your underlined parts again. Look for a phrase that means 'visit several times'. This will help you find the text that says the same thing as question **8** but in different words.

5   Answer the questions about question **9**.
    a   Read all the texts quickly. Underline anything the people say that you think is about the idea of museums changing their exhibitions.
    b   Read your underlined parts again. Which of the texts says the same thing as question **9** but in different words?
    c   Which text contains the word 'exhibition'. Does this bit of text have the idea of the exhibition changing?

6   Continue like this for questions **10**, **11**, **12** and **13**. Read each question carefully then find and underline the parts of the texts that match the question.

7   Now do the exam task for Part 2.

Part 2

Questions 7 – 13

For each question, choose the correct answer.

		Chris	Emily	Daniel
7	Who always visits museums when they travel?	A	B	C
8	Who says it is important to visit the same museum several times?	A	B	C
9	Who likes museums where the exhibitions often change?	A	B	C
10	Who says that museums should have friendly staff?	A	B	C
11	Who says that they sometimes only look at a few things in a room?	A	B	C
12	Who learns more in a museum than in a classroom?	A	B	C
13	Who prefers going around a museum with a guide to going alone?	A	B	C

How important are museums to you?

We asked three young people this question and this is what they told us.

Chris

A lot of my friends think museums are boring but I love them. I prefer ones where they move things round regularly, and bring in new things to keep it interesting. I also like to have things to listen to as well as look at. I suppose I like museums because I'm really interested in history and art. We study these subjects at college, but I've actually found out a lot more about them from museums than from my textbooks.

Emily

I'm lucky because I live in New York, so there are lots of great museums for me to visit. One thing I've learnt is that you should never try to see a whole museum the first time you go. Just go to one or two rooms, and then return as often as you can to see the rest. For me, it's important that the people who work in the museum are pleasant, and happy to talk to me about the things in the exhibition. That makes a big difference.

Daniel

I don't go to museums much, except during my holidays in new cities. Then I make sure I spend at least a day going to the most famous ones. If it's a big museum and I don't have much time, I sometimes walk into a room and choose just five things to look at. I also take a tour if there is one, as I learn so much more from listening to the person showing us round than I do if I'm by myself.

PART 3: TRAINING

Focus on the instructions

1. Look at the exam task on page 16 and 17.
   a What do you have to do in this task?
   b What kind of text is this? Where might you see it?
   c What kind of questions does this part have?
   d How many questions are there?

2. Look at the bullet points below. Tick (✓) the things you think will be in the article. Can you guess two more things that might be in the article?
   - what hill running is
   - how old Jay is
   - who Jay does it with
   - competitions Jay enters
   - how good Jay is
   - injuries Jay has had

3. Read the text quickly to check your answers to 2 above.

Focus on the questions

1. Look at question 14. Read the question and the options carefully. Do you need to answer a question or complete a sentence?

2. Now read question 14 again. Answer these questions about it.
   a There is something about all three options, in the text. Find the information about options A, B and C in this extract from it.

   It's not popular among my friends, but I love it. My dad took me and my brothers out running when we were little, and then when I was about 15 I joined a hill running club, called the York Merlins.

   b The question asks about Jay's first experience of hill running. The answer is C – his family. Why?
   c Why are options A and B wrong?

3. Look at question 15. Read it carefully, and the options. Do you need to answer a question or complete a sentence?

4. Now read question 15 again. Answer these questions about it.
   a The question asks how Jay feels about the good runners in his club. Look at the extract from text below. Is Jay as good as some other runners? Is he upset about this or not? Which phrase tells you this?

   There are some excellent runners in the club. When we do our practice runs, I'm always a long way behind them. But that doesn't bother me. They're all really nice and often give me advice. What I love is being outdoors and finding all these beautiful places I never knew were there.

   b The correct answer is B – he doesn't mind. Why?
   c Why are answers A and C wrong?

5. Now do the same for questions 16, 17 and 18. Underline the important information and then think carefully about the meaning of the question and text before you choose the right answer.

Part 3

Questions 14 – 18

For each question, choose the correct answer.

How I spend my free time
Jay Portman describes his unusual hobby, hill running, and tells us why he enjoys it.

Hill running is the sport of running up and down hills and mountains, through open countryside. It's not popular among my friends, but I love it. My dad took me and my brothers out running when we were little, and then when I was about fifteen, I joined a hill running club, called the York Merlins.

There are some excellent runners in the club. When we do our practice runs, I'm always a long way behind them. But that doesn't bother me. They're all really nice and often give me advice. What I love is being outdoors and finding all these beautiful places I never knew were there.

We race against other clubs at the weekends. In these races, runners are told where to finish, but not how to get there. You need a good map and compass so you don't get lost. Everyone starts together at the beginning, but later in the race you often find yourself running alone.

Anyone can enter these races – you just get there in the morning, pay your £5, and run. There are no T-shirts or medals for the winners. The most you get is a piece of cake! Often there are international hill running champions taking part, but they are just as friendly as everyone else.

That doesn't mean it's an easy sport. Last weekend I did a race in heavy rain and high winds, and I was asking myself what I was doing out there. But I got to the end, and that was an amazing feeling.

14 Jay's first experience of hill running was with

　A　a club.

　B　some friends.

　C　his family.

15 How does Jay feel about the good runners in his club?

　A　He'd like to be as fast as them one day.

　B　He doesn't mind that they are better than him.

　C　He thinks they should help slower runners improve.

16 What does Jay say is important in the races he enters?

　A　listening to the instructions

　B　staying close to other runners

　C　being able to find your way

17 What do we learn about the races from the fourth paragraph?

　A　They don't have big prizes.

　B　They are only for local runners.

　C　They are free for some people to enter.

18 What does Jay say about the last race he did?

　A　The bad weather made it dangerous.

　B　He was very happy when he finished it.

　C　It wasn't as difficult as some races he has done.

PART 4: TRAINING

Focus on the instructions

1. Look at the exam task on page 19.
   a What do you have to do in this task?
   b What kind of text is this? Where might you see it?
   c What kind of questions does this part have?
   d How many questions are there?

2. Look at the title of the text and the photo. What kind of information do you think the text will include? Tick (✓) what you expect to read about.
   - when Dakota Fanning was born ☐
   - what her family does ☐
   - the films she has been in ☐
   - her first acting job ☐
   - where she lives now ☐

3. Read the text once. Don't worry about the gaps yet. Check your answers to 2.

Focus on the questions

1. Look at question **19**. All of these words can be about someone's age, but only one fits in this sentence. We can say *a little girl* and *a small girl*, but can we say *a little age* or *a small age*?

2. Now look at question **20**. All of these words are about work, but only one fits in this sentence. The important words here are *long and successful*. Is it possible to have *a long job* or *a long occupation*?

Focus on the language

1. Some words, like *career*, *job* and *occupation* have a similar meaning but they are not used in the same way.
   Choose the best word to complete each gap. Put the word in its correct form.
   a arrive/drive/travel
      i 'John always .... late in the morning,' said his teacher.
      ii Penny .... to school by bus.
      iii Louise's mum .... her to school every morning.
   b do/make/play
      i All she does is .... computer games all day.
      ii Every evening I help to .... the washing-up.
      iii Paul .... his bed every morning before he goes to school.
   c look/see/watch
      i Did you .... TV last night?
      ii I .... my friend at the cinema last night.
      iii Jane has .... everywhere for her keys, but she can't find them.
   d decide/plan/think
      i Next summer we .... to visit my cousins in South Africa.
      ii I .... I'll call Rob.
      iii I've .... to write a story about my last holiday.

2. Now look at questions **19–24** on page 19 and choose the correct answers.

Part 4

Questions 19 – 24

For each question, choose the correct answer.

Dakota Fanning

Dakota Fanning was born on February 23rd 1994, in Georgia, USA. She began acting classes at a very **(19)**............... age and starred in her first TV advert when she was just five years old.

After that, she had a long and successful **(20)**............... as a child actor in both TV shows and films. In 2001, she **(21)**............... an important prize for her part in the film *I am Sam*. Over the next ten years, she acted with many big Hollywood stars, including Reese Witherspoon, Tom Cruise and Kurt Russell.

Dakota Fanning is different from many child actors because her success continued as she **(22)**............... up and became an adult. In 2018, she **(23)**............... to TV for the first time in ten years, starring in a popular police drama set in the nineteenth century, **(24)**............... *The Alienist*.

19	A	small	B	early	C	little
20	A	career	B	job	C	occupation
21	A	did	B	earned	C	won
22	A	got	B	grew	C	went
23	A	returned	B	changed	C	arrived
24	A	said	B	told	C	called

PART 5: TRAINING

Focus on the instructions

1. Look at the exam task on page 21.
   a. What do you have to do in this task?
   b. How many questions are there?
   c. What kind of text is this?
   d. Is this part testing your knowledge of grammar or vocabulary?

2. Read the email.
   Do you think Tom and Rob are friends?
   Why is Tom writing to Rob?

Focus on the questions

1. The kind of words tested in this part are grammar words. Look at the example. What kind of word is *about*?

2. Look at question **25**. Which word do we use with *thanks so …* to mean 'a lot'?

3. Look at the sentence with question **26**. What is the function of this sentence? Which question word is needed?

4. Now look at question **27**. You need a preposition here. Why is *before* wrong? Which is the correct preposition?

5. Look at question **28**. What word can we use with *are* at the beginning of this sentence?

6. Look at question **29**. What kind of word must follow *wanted to* in question 29? Which word completes the phrase *…. someone know*?

7. Now look at question **30**. What kind of word must follow *It will …*? What form must it be in? What is the word needed here?

Focus on the language

1. Complete the gaps with a preposition from the box.

   | at | by | in | on | on | to | to |

   a. Let's meet .... 6.00 o'clock.
   b. I usually go to school .... foot but today I came .... bus.
   c. I was born .... the 11th October.
   d. Do you go .... primary school?
   e. What time do you wake up .... the morning?
   f. Can I speak .... you, please?

2. Choose the best option to complete each sentence.
   a. Is that jumper *your / yours*?
   b. *Here / There* are many people outside.
   c. I have so *many / much* friends – at least twenty!
   d. *Lots / Some* people think maths is hard but I don't.
   e. Have we got *a / any* sugar?

3. Choose the best option to complete each question.
   a. *What / How* is your brother called?
   b. What *did / are* Miss Jones tell you?
   c. *Have / Did* you seen Toby today?
   d. *How / Where* about going shopping?

4. Think of one verb to complete each sentence. Sometimes more than one answer is possible.
   a. I .... you can come and see me soon.
   b. Let me .... if you can come.
   c. I want to .... swimming later.
   d. I'd .... to see you later.
   e. I .... free this morning but not this afternoon.

PART 5: TRAINING READING AND WRITING

Part 5

Questions 25 – 30

For each question, write the correct answer. Write **one** word for each gap.

Example: | 0 | about |

New Message

From: Tom
To: Rob

I'm writing | 0 | about | my party on Saturday. Thanks so | 25 | for offering to help me get everything ready. | 26 | don't you come over to my place tomorrow | 27 | school? We can have dinner together and start planning. | 28 | are lots of things to think about!

Also, I wanted to | 29 | you know that I'm going to invite a girl called Hannah to the party. She's just moved into the house next door to mine, so it will | 30 | a good way for her to meet people and make friends.

Text me if you can come tomorrow.

PART 6: TRAINING

Focus on the instructions

1. Look at the exam task on page 23.
   a What type of text do you need to write?
   b Who must you write to?
   c What three pieces of information must you include?

Focus on the questions

1. Read the three answers to the exam question and for each one, answer these questions.
   a Has the student included something about all three pieces of information?
   b Has the student written enough words?
   c Is the answer easy to understand?
   d Are there any language mistakes in the answer?

   1
   Dear Ashley,
   I got nice clothses to go the shops, you like it I know. You can come with me on Saturday for shopping? It's great. Call soon, my friend.
   Paul

   2
   Hi Ashley,
   Would you like come shoping with me on Saturday, if you are free? I need to get some new clothes because I am going in holiday at two weeks. I want to going to the new shopping center in town.
   Let me know,
   Jose

   3
   Ashley,
   I need to go shops for new cloths. Mines are all very small now as I am grow too fast. I'm going to department store in the town. I like cloths in there.
   Tania

2. Match the students' answers in exercise 2 with the examiner's comments below.
   A This is a very good answer. All the information is included. The organisation is good, with some examples of conjunctions. There are a few small mistakes with grammar and spelling, but they don't stop the reader fully understanding the message.

   B This is a very poor answer. Only the invitation is included – the rest is impossible to understand.

   C This answer is okay, but not very good. One point is missing – there is no invitation included. The other two points are included. There are some mistakes with spelling and grammar.

3. Write your own answer to the writing task.

Part 6

Question 31

You want to go shopping for some new clothes on Saturday.

Write an email to your English friend, Ashley.

In your email:
- **ask** Ashley to come with you
- **explain why** you need new clothes
- **say where** you'd like to go shopping.

Write **25 words** or more.

PART 7: TRAINING

Focus on the instructions

1. Look at the exam task on page 25.
   a. What type of text do you need to write?
   b. What information must you include?

Focus on the questions

1. Read the three answers to the exam question and for each one, answer these questions.
   a. Has the student included something about all three pictures?
   b. Has the student written enough words?
   c. Is the answer easy to understand?
   d. Are there any language mistakes in the answer?

   1. Jane and Susan love the music so going to a concert in the park. They show their tickets to the staff at the gate and walk inside. They has the picnic on the grass before the concert. They eating sandwiches and drinks. When the music start they danced and have a great time.

   2. Me and my friend arrived at the park and gave our tickets at the gate. We waited for the music and when the band played we danced and sang all the songs. It was the best day of our lives.

   3. We give our tickets and then entered the park and had picnic. Then we dance to the music.

2. Match the answers with the examiner's comments and scores below.
   A. This is a good answer. Information from all the pictures is included. The organisation is good, with lots of examples of good organisation of ideas – *so*, *and*, *before* and *when*. There are some mistakes with tenses which make it a bit difficult to understand in places.
   B. This is a poor answer. It does tell the story shown in the pictures, but it is too short – it is only 18 words and it should be at least 35.
   C. This answer is okay but not very good. One point is missing – there is no mention of the picnic. The other two points are included and clear.

3. Write your own answer for the writing task.

Part 7

Question 32

Look at the three pictures.

Write the story shown in the pictures.

Write **35 words** or more.

OVERVIEW
PAPER 2: LISTENING

About the paper

The Listening paper lasts about 30 minutes. This includes 6 minutes for you to write your answers on the Answer Sheet.

There are five parts in the Listening test. In Parts 1 and 4, you hear short recordings and answer one question with three options on each recording. In Part 2, you hear one long recording and you have to write down five pieces of information. In Part 3, you hear a long recording and you have to answer five three-option multiple-choice questions. In Part 5, you have to answer five matching questions. You hear each recording twice.

There are five parts to the Listening paper which is 25% of your overall score. Each part has five questions in it and is worth 5 marks.

How to do the paper

Part 1
You hear five different short recordings and you have to answer a question about each one. You always hear two people talking about something in an everyday situation. For each question, there are three pictures. You read the question, listen to the recording and decide which picture is the correct answer. You have to listen for specific information in the conversation, such as times, places, activities and plans. Listen carefully, because you hear about the things in all three pictures, but only one picture answers the question.

Part 2
In Part 2, there is one long recording and there is always just one person talking. For example, you may hear a teacher giving her class some information. You hear a sentence that tells you who is speaking and what they're talking about. You then have time to read a set of notes from which some of the information is missing. The task begins with an example. Read this carefully and think about the type of information you need to fill each of the five gaps.

When you listen, follow the information in the notes. You will hear some of the words that are written there. Be ready to write the missing information in the gaps. Write the exact word, number, date or time that you hear. Always listen carefully. You may hear more than one word that could fit in a gap, but only one word is the correct answer. Sometimes, you have to write the spelling of a word, like somebody's name for example. Listen to the letters carefully.

PARTS 1–5 LISTENING

Part 3
In Part 3, there is also one long recording, but this time it's a conversation between two people. You hear and read a sentence that tells you who is speaking and what they are talking about. For example, it could be two friends talking about a concert they have just been to. You then have time to read the five three-option multiple-choice questions. The information in the recording comes in the same order as the questions.

You listen and choose the correct answer (**A**, **B** or **C**). Listen carefully and think about the meaning of what the people say. You may not always hear the same words that are written in the options, but you do hear the answer to the question.

Part 4
In Part 4, you hear five short recordings. You may hear just one person speaking or it may be a conversation between two people. There is a multiple-choice question for each recording.

You hear a sentence that tells you who is speaking and what they are talking about. Then you have time to read the question and the options (**A**, **B** and **C**). You listen to the recording and choose the correct answer. You need to listen for the main idea or topic. You do not usually hear the same words that you read in the options, so think about the meaning of what the people are saying.

Some questions ask about one of the people, but others may ask about both. Sometimes the question might ask, for example, why the speakers didn't go somewhere or didn't enjoy something. Always read the question carefully.

Part 5
In Part 5, you hear one long recording and you have to match items in one list with items in another list. There are always two people speaking. There are five questions and seven options. There is an example at the beginning so you see eight options, **A–H**, on the page.

You hear and read a sentence that tells you who is speaking and what they are talking about, for example, it may be a boy telling a friend about the postcards he got from different people. You listen and choose the correct answer (**A–H**). Listen carefully and think about the meaning of what the people say. You may not always hear the same words that are written in the options. Sometimes you may hear two words that are options, but only one answers the question correctly.

LISTENING **OVERVIEW**

PART 1: TRAINING

Focus on the instructions

1 Look at the task on pages 30 and 31.
   a How many questions are there?
   b How many pictures does each question have?
   c What do you have to do?

Focus on the questions

1 Look at question **1**. What information must you listen for?

2 🔊 Now read question **1** and listen to the recording. Underline the times in the extract from the audio script.

   Question 1. What time will Josh and Hannah meet?

   Josh: Hi Hannah. Don't forget we're going to the cinema for Lucy's birthday tonight.

   Hannah: I know Josh! Shall we go together? We can catch the seven o'clock bus from Grange Road.

   Josh: OK. I'll come to your house at a quarter to seven and we can walk to the bus stop from there.

   Hannah: Great. But don't be late! The film starts at half past seven.

3 Match each time to one of the the pictures, **A**, **B** or **C**.

A   B   C

4 Read question **1** again carefully. Underline the text in the recording that matches the meaning of the question.

5 Which time answers the question correctly?

6 Why are the other two options wrong?

7 Now look at the question and pictures for question **2**. What does the £ symbol mean?

8 🔊 Prices, times and other numbers are often tested in Part 1. Listen and tick (✓) the correct price, time or number that you hear.

1	**A** 5	☐	**B** 25	☐
2	**A** 330	☐	**B** 303	☐
3	**A** £14	☐	**B** £40	☐
4	**A** £5.99	☐	**B** £599	☐
5	**A** 6.45	☐	**B** 7.15	☐
6	**A** 7.20 a.m.	☐	**B** 7.20 p.m.	☐

9 Describe the covers of the notebooks in the pictures for question **3**. How are they different?

10 Now read question **4** and name the sports in the pictures.

11 🔊 Listen and check your answers to question **4**.

12 Read the question and name the kinds of food in the pictures for question **5**.

13 🔊 Now read question **5** and listen to the recording. Answer these questions.
   a What is the girl's dad planning for dinner?
   b what did the girl have for her lunch?
   c What does the girl want for dinner?

Question 5. What will the girl eat for dinner tonight?

Girl: Hi Dad. What's that you're cooking?

Dad: It's roast chicken for our dinner.

Girl: Do you mind if I have something else? I had a big plate of pasta at school so I'm not very hungry.

Dad: No problem. There's some soup in the fridge.

Girl: Perfect! I'll have the chicken tomorrow.

14 Now try the exam task.

Part 1

Questions 1 – 5

For each question, choose the correct answer.

1 What time will Josh and Hannah meet?

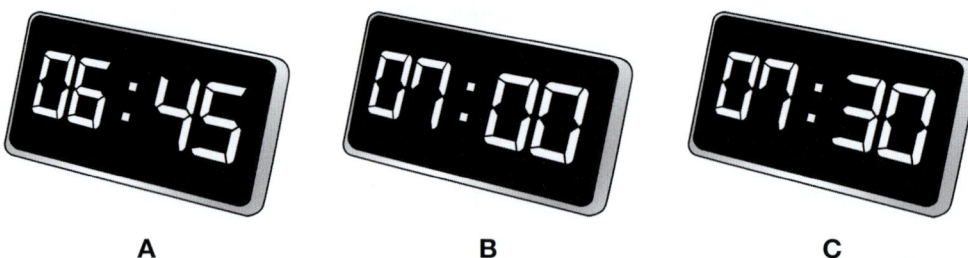

A   B   C

2 How much did the girl pay for her tennis shoes?

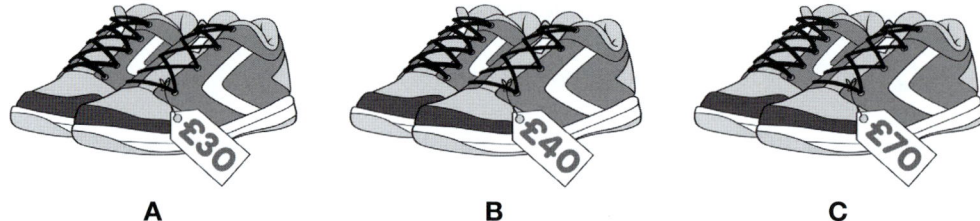

A   B   C

3 Which notebook was left in the classroom?

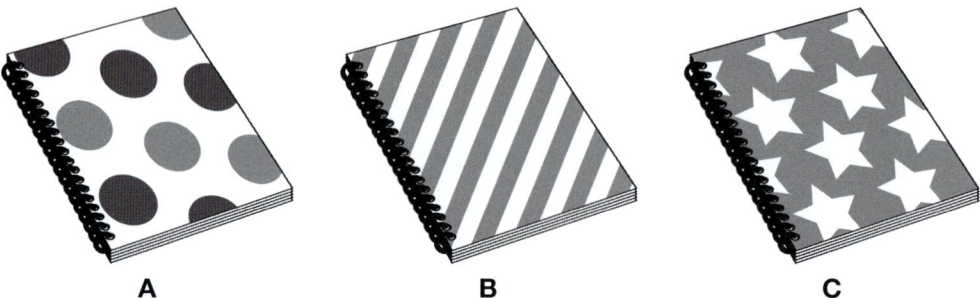

A   B   C

4 Which after-school sport will the boy do this term?

A B C

5 What will the girl eat for dinner tonight?

A B C

PART 2: TRAINING

Focus on the instructions

1 Look at the exam task on page 33.
   a How many questions are there?
   b Who will you hear? What will the person talk about?
   c What do you have to do?

Focus on the questions

1 Read the notes for Part 2. What kind of information is missing? Match the questions with **A–F**.

   Example
   Question 6
   Question 7
   Question 8
   Question 9
   Question 10

   A a thing
   B a time
   C a name
   D a day of the week
   E a phone number
   F a date

   (Example matched to F a date)

2 🔊 Listen to the recording. Write down the phone numbers you hear.
   a ....
   b ....
   c ....
   d ....

3 In pairs, practise reading out the phone numbers in exercise 2.

4 🔊 Listen to some people spelling their names. Write the names that you hear.
   a ....
   b ....
   c ....
   d ....
   e ....

5 Work in pairs. Ask your partner to spell the following names:
   a Your name
   ....
   b Your dad's/mum's name
   ....
   c Your best friend's name
   ....
   d Your grandmother's name
   ....
   e The name of your town/village
   ....

6 🔊 Read these dates. Then listen and repeat.
   a 20th November
   b 2nd November
   c 12th November
   d 1st December
   e 25th March
   f 31st May

7 Now try the exam task.

Part 2

Questions 6 – 10

For each question, write the correct answer in the gap. Write **one word** or **a number** or **a date** or **a time**.

You will hear a girl leaving a message about band practice.

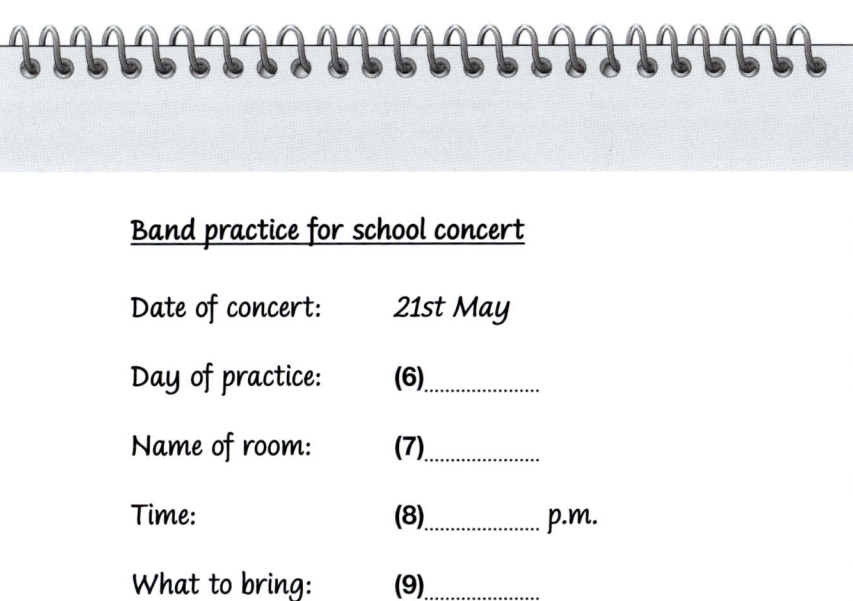

Band practice for school concert

Date of concert: 21st May

Day of practice: (6) ....

Name of room: (7) ....

Time: (8) .... p.m.

What to bring: (9) ....

Number to call: (10) ....

PART 3: TRAINING

Focus on the instructions

1 Look at the exam task on page 35.
 a How many questions are there?
 b Who will you hear? What will they talk about?
 c What do you have to do?

Focus on the questions

1 Read through all the questions carefully. Choose which speaker you think will give the answer for each question.

 Question 11   Darren / Maria
 Question 12   Darren / Maria
 Question 13   Darren / Maria
 Question 14   Darren / Maria
 Question 15   Darren / Maria

2 Which questions are about facts and which are about opinions or feelings?

3 Match the sentences with the feelings and opinions.
 1 'The book had 600 pages and I couldn't finish it.'
 2 'I enjoyed horse-riding more than anything else.'
 3 'I don't want to go to the party because I won't know anyone.'
 4 'The film made me laugh a lot.'
 5 'There isn't enough light in this room.'
 6 'I can't wait to go to the theatre.'

 A It's too dark.
 B It was my favourite activity.
 C It was very long.
 D I'm excited about going there.
 E It was funny.
 F I'm worried about going there.

4 Now read question 11 and listen to the first part of the conversation. Answer the questions about it.

 Question 11. The dance school Maria goes to is
 A near her home.
 B in the town centre.
 C at her college.

 Darren: You're looking well Maria. Are you still doing a lot of running?
 Maria: Actually, I've started going to a dance school. It's great for me because I can get the bus there from the town centre after college, and then it's just a short walk to my house when the lesson ends.

 a The answer to question 11 is A – near her home. Underline the information that tells us this in the audioscript.
 b Why is B wrong?
 c Why is C wrong?

5 Now try the exam task.

Part 3

Questions 11 – 15

For each question, choose the correct answer.

You will hear Maria talking to her friend Darren about a dance school.

11 The dance school Maria goes to is

    A   near her home.

    B   in the town centre.

    C   at her college.

12 What kind of dance is Maria learning at the moment?

    A   modern dance

    B   street dance

    C   jazz dance

13 How much did Maria pay for her dance classes?

    A   £25

    B   £75

    C   £100

14 Why does Darren want to do dance classes?

    A   to get fit

    B   to have fun

    C   to make new friends

15 Darren agrees to meet Maria next Saturday

    A   at the bus stop.

    B   at Maria's home.

    C   at the dance school.

PART 4: TRAINING

TEST 1 — LISTENING

Focus on the instructions

1. Look at the exam task on page 37.
   a How many questions are there?
   b What do you have to do?

2. This part tests your understanding of gist and not detail. Which of these are gist and which are detail? Write G (gist) or D (detail).
   a a date ....
   b an opinion or feeling ....
   c a price ....
   d the general subject ....
   e the reason for speaking ....
   f a time ....
   g a number ....
   h understanding where people are ....

Focus on the questions

1. Now read questions **16–20**. Match each one with the question types in Exercise 2 above.

2. 🔊 Read question **16** then read and listen to the extract from the audioscript. Answer the questions about it.

   Question 16. You will hear two friends talking. Where are they?
   A   at home
   B   in a restaurant
   C   on a train.

   Girl: I'm really hungry! I forgot to eat before <u>we left the house</u>.
   Boy: Me too, I'm starving! And we won't <u>get to our station</u> for another two hours.
   Girl: How much money have you got on you?
   Boy: Six pounds. It's enough to get a couple of sandwiches.
   Girl: OK. You go and get them. <u>I'll stay in my seat and look after our bags.</u>

   a Look at the underlined information in the audioscript and the three options. Which is the right answer?
   b Why is **A** wrong? Which of the underlined sentences tells you this?
   c The two people talk about food, so why is **B** wrong? Underline the sentence which tells you this.

3. Now try the exam task.

Part 4

Questions 16 – 20

For each question, choose the correct answer.

16 You will hear two friends talking. Where are they?

    A   at home

    B   in a restaurant

    C   on a train

17 You will hear two friends talking in a clothes shop. What doesn't the man like about the jacket?

    A   its colour

    B   its price

    C   its length

18 You will hear a woman talking on the radio. What is she doing?

    A   giving instructions

    B   describing a meal

    C   offering advice

19 You will hear two friends talking at home. What have they just broken?

    A   a game

    B   a glass

    C   some furniture

20 You will hear a man describing a painting. What is the painting of?

    A   a street

    B   a forest

    C   a person

PART 5: TRAINING

Focus on the instructions

1 Look at the exam task on page 39.
   a How many people will you hear?
   b What will they talk about?
   c How many questions are there?
   d What do you have to do?
   e How many answers are there that you will not use?

Focus on the questions

1 🔊 Read and listen to the first part of the conversation, and look at the example in the task on page 39. Now look at the underlined text in the extract from the conversation. This gives the answer to the example. Can you explain why?

   Laura: What are you doing over the holidays, Pete?

   Pete: <u>On Monday, nothing, except sleep! I'm so tired.</u>

   Laura: ha, ha! What about Tuesday?

   Pete: Well, my friend is coming to stay with me for a few days, so I want to get all my school work done that day, before he arrives. I've got a lot of maths and French to do.

2 🔊 Look at question 21. Read and listen to the first part of the conversation again. You must match a plan from the list **A–H** with the day, *Tuesday*. Answer these questions about question 21.
   a Does the word Tuesday come before or after the plan?
   b The correct answer is **G**. Underline the words that tell you this.
   c Why is **H** wrong?

3 Now try the exam task.

PART 5: TRAINING LISTENING

Part 5

Questions 21 – 25

For each question, choose the correct answer.

You will hear Pete talking to a friend about his holiday plans.

What is his plan for each day?

Example:

0   Monday | E |

Days

21   Tuesday | |

22   Wednesday | |

23   Thursday | |

24   Friday | |

25   Saturday | |

Plans

A   do some sport

B   go shopping

C   go sightseeing

D   go to the theatre

E   rest

F   see a film

G   study

H   visit a friend

OVERVIEW
PAPER 3: SPEAKING

About the paper

The Speaking test lasts between 8 and 10 minutes and there are two parts. There are two examiners; one speaks to you and the other one just listens. You do the test with a partner. In some parts you talk to the examiner and in other parts you talk to each other.

The examiners give you marks for the test as a whole. They use a mark scheme to decide which band your answer falls in. There are four categories: global achievement, grammar and vocabulary, pronunciation, and interactive communication. For each of these you will get a mark out of 5. Your score out of 20 is adjusted to give marks out of 25.

Your speaking does not have to be perfect to get full marks. However, you go down one or more bands if your speaking is hard to understand, if you don't say enough, or if you do not show the examiners that you know a wide enough range of grammar and vocabulary at A2 level.

How to do the paper

Part 1

In Part 1, the examiner asks each of you questions about yourselves. You speak to the examiner in this part, and not to each other. The first few questions are simple ones, for example, your name, where you come from and, perhaps, your age. You just give short simple answers to these questions.

After this, the examiner asks each of you more questions on everyday topics, for example, ways of travelling or what you do at the weekend. You only need to give short answers to these questions. The examiner will also ask each of you a question which starts 'Please tell me something about …' and you should give a longer answer to this question.

Part 2

In Part 2, you speak to your partner. The examiner gives you a page with five pictures on it. These will show things or activities, such as ways of travelling or different sports. The examiner asks you to talk to your partner about whether you like or don't like the things or activities. You should give your reasons.

The examiner then asks some questions about some or all of the pictures. You might have to say, for example, if you think the thing or activity is interesting, exciting or boring.

Finally, the examiner asks each of you two more questions on the same topic. You should give reasons for your answers.

See **SPEAKING BANK** for useful language and practice
See **GRAMMAR BANK** for reference and practice

PART 1: TRAINING

Focus on the instructions

1. Look at Part 1 Phase 1 on page 43. Do you have to take turns or talk with your partner?

2. Now look at Part 1 Phase 2. Do you answer the same questions as your partner or different ones?

Focus on the questions

1. Read the Part 1 Phase 1 questions on page 43. Answer the questions.
   a Is this part asking you about your personal details or your feelings?
   b Do the questions look simple or difficult?

2. Ask and answer the Part 1 Phase 1 questions on page 43 with your partner.

3. Now read the Part 1 Phase 2 questions. Answer the questions.
   a How many topics will you talk about in Part 1 Phase 2
   b How many questions must each of you answer?
   c Which question needs a longer answer?

4. Ask and answer the Part 1 Phase 2 questions on page 43 with your partner.

Focus on the language

1. In Part 1 you have to give personal information. Look at these typical Part 1 questions and match them to the answers.

   1 What's your name?
   2 Where do you live?
   3 Tell me something about your school.
   4 How old are you?
   5 What do you do in your free time?
   6 How often do you play football?
   7 Which subject do you like best? Why?
   8 Which subject is the most difficult?
   9 Do you work or are you a student?

   A Chemistry, because I don't understand it
   B I'm 13.
   C It's quite large. We don't have to wear a uniform, but we get a lot of homework.
   D I'm a student.
   E Every Sunday.
   F I play football and I watch TV.
   G In Madrid.
   H My name's Fabio.
   I Maths, because it's easier than the other subjects.

Part 1 (3–4 minutes)

Phase 1

The examiner will ask you and your partner some questions about yourself.
- What's your name?
- How old are you?
- Do you work or are you a student?
- Where do you come from?
- Where do you live?

Phase 2

Now, let's talk about **food**.

A, what do you usually have for breakfast?
How often do you go to cafés or restaurants?

B, where do you eat lunch at weekends?
In your family, who cooks the best food?

Extended response
Now **A**, please tell me something about your dinner yesterday.

Extra questions
Where did you have dinner?
Who did you eat with?
What did you eat?

Now, let's talk about **evenings**.
B, how often do you go out in the evening?
What work or studying do you do in the evening?

A, what do you like doing best in the evening?
When do you usually go to bed?

Extended response
Now **B**, please tell me something about what you will do this evening.

Extra questions
Where will you spend this evening?
Will you play computer games this evening?
How do you think you will feel at the end of this evening?

PART 2: TRAINING

Focus on the instructions

1 Look at the first paragraph of Part 2 Phase 1 on page 45.
   a Who will you talk to in this part of the test?
   b What will the examiner give you?

2 Now look at Part 2 Phase 2.
   a What kind of questions do you answer in Part 2 Phase 2?
   b How many questions must you answer?
   c Do you answer the same questions as your partner or different ones?

Focus on the questions

1 Look at the pictures for Phase 1 on page 162.
   a What is the topic of the pictures?
   b What does each picture show?

2 Now look at the examiner's questions in Part 2 Phase 1. Which questions are about your opinion? Which question is about your preference?

3 Speak about the pictures for 1–2 minutes with your partner.

4 Look at the questions beginning 'Do you think …'
   1 Underline the adjectives and check you understand all of them.
   2 Think about your answers to these questions. How many will you answer 'Yes' to and how many will you answer 'No' to?
   3 Think of some reasons for your answers.

5 Choose two or three questions to ask your partner from Phase 2. Answer your partner's questions.

Focus on the language

1 Look at these ways of saying if you like or don't like something. Match them with the emoticons.

I hate …	A
I don't mind …	B
I don't really like …	C
I really love …	D
I like …	E
I quite like …	F

2 Which of the following can you say if you haven't understood something? Which two should you not say? Why not?
   a *Sorry, I don't understand. Can you say that again?*
   b *What?*
   c *I don't understand you!*
   d *Can you please repeat your question?*
   e *I'm sorry. Please can you repeat that?*
   f *What do you mean? Can you explain?*

Part 2 (5–6 minutes)

Phase 1

The examiner will show you some pictures and ask you and your partner to talk about the things they show.
Now, in this part of the test you are going to talk together.
(Turn to the pictures on page 164.)

Here are some pictures that show different **sports**.

Do you like these different sports? Say why or why not. I'll say that again.
Do you like these different sports? Say why or why not.
All right? Now, talk together.

⏲ about 1–2 minutes

The examiner will ask you at least one question each.

Do you think …

… playing basketball is fun?
… sailing is expensive?
… running in a race is hard?
… riding a horse is easy?
… cycling is good for you?

Extra questions
Why?/Why not?
What do you think?

So, **A**, which of these sports do you like best?
And you, **B**, which of these sports do you like best?

⏲ about 1–2 minutes

Thank you.

Phase 2

Now, which is more interesting, playing sports or watching sports, **B**? (Why?)
And what about you, **A**? (Which is more interesting, playing sports or watching sports?) (Why?)

Did you enjoy sport when you were at school, **A**? (Why?/Why not?)
And you, **B**? (Did you enjoy sport when you were at school?) (Why?/Why not?)

⏲ maximum 2 minutes

Thank you. That is the end of the test.

TEST 2

Part 1

Questions 1 – 6

For each question, choose the correct answer.

1

School Library
Use your student card to borrow books
Only five books per student

A No student can take more than five books out of the library.

B If you need more than five books you must get a student card.

C Five students still need to collect their books from the school library.

2

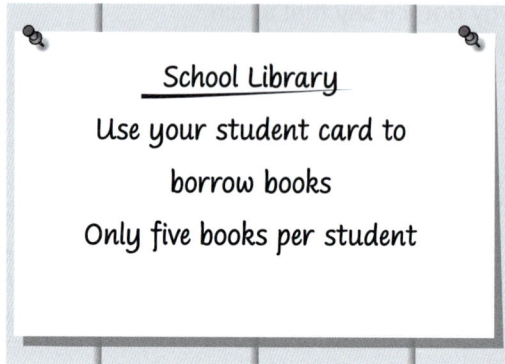

Greenview School
Cycling allowed, but students may not use skateboards to get to school.

This notice gives students information about

A where to leave cycles and skateboards.

B why skateboards are dangerous.

C how they can travel to school.

3

Boats for hire
30 mins
Adults £3.00
Children £2.00
Full safety details in office

A Each child must have an adult with them.

B There is more information to read indoors.

C Find out about prices in the office.

TIP STRIP

Question 1: What does the notice say about 'five books'? Which option matches this sentence?

Question 2: What does 'to get to school' mean? Find an option that has this meaning, in different words.

Question 3: Read the options carefully. What does the notice say about adults/children and prices? Do options A and C match this?

4

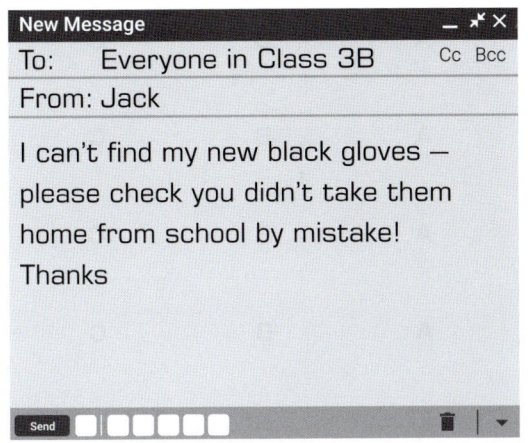

Where does Jack think his gloves are?

A   in the classroom

B   at his home

C   with one of his friends

5

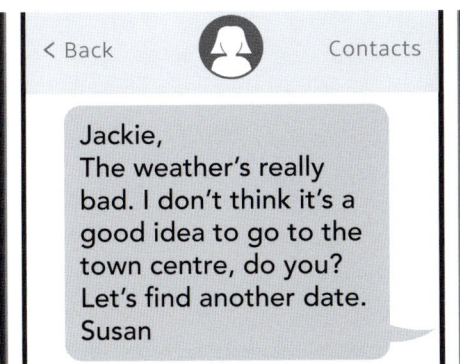

What is Susan doing in this message?

A   offering to go shopping with Jackie

B   suggesting she and Jackie change their plan

C   asking Jackie where they should meet each other

6

Longdrive Football Club

You must pay by this Friday to continue being a member next year.

Forms available from the manager's office

What must club members decide?

A   where to keep important documents

B   how much new members should pay

C   if they want to stay at the club

TIP STRIP

Question 4: Who is Jack writing to? What does he think has happened to his gloves?

Question 5: Read the message carefully. What plan did Jackie and Susan have? What is the problem? What does Susan want to do?

Question 6: Read the notice. What does it say about paying and about the forms? What will happen if members do not pay by Friday?

Part 2

Questions 7 – 13

For each question, choose the correct answer.

		Active Art	Dance!	You and Me
7	Which show is on twice a week?	A	B	C
8	Which show is about a group of friends?	A	B	C
9	Which show teaches you how to do something?	A	B	C
10	Which show is a comedy?	A	B	C
11	Which show is about someone who wants to change her life?	A	B	C
12	Which show has a well-known star?	A	B	C
13	Which show is good for people of all ages?	A	B	C

TIP STRIP

You may find information about a topic in more than one text, but only one text will answer the question correctly.

Question 7: Be careful! The word 'twice' is in text **C**, but does this bit of information answer the question?

Question 8: What does 'They become close' mean in text **B**?

Question 9: Which two texts have information about teaching and learning? Which one gives the answer to this question?

Question 10: Which two shows will make you laugh? What is a 'comedy'? What kind of show is *Active Art*?

Question 11: Which two shows are about a girl? Which of these girls wants a different kind of life?

Question 12: One text mentions 'a big star' and another has the phrase 'world-famous'. Read these sections carefully and decide which gives you the answer to the question.

Question 13: Find the information in each text about who the show is for. Find a phrase that has a similar meaning to 'people of all ages'.

Three great TV shows

A *Active Art*

Active Art is a new show for 12–15-year-olds. Each week, the world-famous artist Tony Moldino shows viewers how to make an amazing work of art. He's great in front of the camera and surprisingly funny. Last week's show was all about painting faces. This week, it's drawing with pencil and next week, it's digital photography. You can see *Active Art* every Tuesday and Thursday at 5.00 p.m.

B *Dance!*

Dance! is a new drama for teenagers, about the lives of teachers and students at a dance school in New York. The most important person in the story is Tina Giles, a young girl from a poor part of town who dreams of becoming a big star. On her first day at the school she meets Joe, Heather and John. They become close and together they have many exciting adventures. *Dance!* is on every Monday night at 7.00.

C *You and Me*

The new series of *You and Me* returns this Saturday at 6.00 p.m. with a special show that's twice as long as usual. This show is perfect for the whole family to watch together, as everyone will find something to laugh at. Each week, we get a different story about the life of Harriet, a high school student. In this week's episode, her younger brother gets a part in the school play. Harriet wants to be in the play too and does everything she can think of to make this happen!

Part 3

Questions 14 – 18

For each question, choose the correct answer.

Playing music in a rock band is a great way to meet people who are interested in the same things as you, and to have a lot of fun. The first thing you'll need to do is decide what instruments you want in your band. Most bands have one or two guitars, a singer, drums and keyboards, but you can change this. However, every band must have drums – you will need someone who can play those.

The next thing is to find your bandmates. Begin by making a poster. Describe the kind of music you want to make and the instruments you want in your band. Put the poster up in your school or college and ask your friends if they know anyone who would like to join.

Once you have a band, you'll need to quickly think of a name. The best way to do this is to spend two hours with your bandmates, writing down hundreds of ideas. Most will be really bad, but there will be a few good ones. Choose something surprising and interesting, that people won't be able to forget.

Next, you'll need to practise as much as you can. You will need a place where you can make a lot of noise without making your neighbours angry. Trying to play quietly will not help you get better. Don't spend time learning songs written by other people. Try writing your own. And don't be afraid of writing about your normal everyday experiences. All bands begin like this.

14 Which instrument does the writer think is most important in a band?

- **A** drums
- **B** guitars
- **C** keyboards

15 What does the writer suggest in the second paragraph?

- **A** listen to your classmates' bands
- **B** advertise in the place where you study
- **C** ask your friends to join your band

16 What does the writer say about choosing a band name?

- **A** Make sure it is easy to remember.
- **B** Be ready to change it if it is not popular.
- **C** Spend a few weeks thinking about it.

17 The writer thinks it is important for new bands to

- **A** write songs about unusual things.
- **B** begin by learning famous songs.
- **C** play loudly when they practise.

18 What is the best title for this article?

- **A** The world's best rock band
- **B** How to start a rock band
- **C** My life in a rock band

TIP STRIP

Question 17: Read the final paragraph carefully. Find the text about practising, learning other band's songs and writing songs. Which information matches the meaning of an option in question 17?

Question 18: Think about the writer's reason for writing this text. Is the writer describing their own band or another band? Is the writer giving advice? If so, which option matches this idea?

Part 4

Questions 19 – 24

For each question, choose the correct answer.

Tasmanian devils

Tasmanian devils are about the size of a small dog. They have a coat of dark fur with a few lighter areas on some **(19)**............... of their bodies. Their heads are large and they have very strong teeth.

In the **(20)**..............., Tasmanian devils lived all over Australia, but today they are only **(21)**............... on the island of Tasmania in the south-east of the country.

Tasmanian devils are meat-eaters and are active at night. They usually eat animals that are already dead, but also catch **(22)**............... like snakes, birds, fish and insects. Like many Australian animals, including the kangaroo, Tasmanian devils are 'marsupials'. This **(23)**............... their babies are very small when they are born. Their mothers carry them in a special pocket **(24)**............... a 'pouch' on the front of their bodies until they are big and strong.

19	A	pieces	B	places	C	parts
20	A	history	B	past	C	century
21	A	found	B	looked	C	watched
22	A	examples	B	things	C	ways
23	A	means	B	decides	C	thinks
24	A	told	B	said	C	called

TIP STRIP

Read through the text carefully to understand what it is about. Then try to answer the questions.

Question 19: Only one of these words completes the phrase. Which one is it?

Question 20: Which word can you use with 'the' to talk generally about 'the time before now'?

Question 21: This sentence tells you where Tasmanian devils live, so which verb is correct?

Question 22: This sentence is giving examples but does the word 'examples' fit in the gap? Can snakes, birds and fish be 'ways'?

Question 23: This sentence is giving a definition of 'marsupial', so which option fits here?

Question 24: Which of these words do you use to give the name of something?

Part 5

Questions 25 – 30

For each question, write the correct answer. Write one word for each gap.

Example: | 0 | are |

New Message

From: Jason
To: Tania

How (0) **are** you? I'm writing to ask about the swimming club you belong to. I'm having swimming lessons at my local pool and my coach says I am now (25) _____ best in the group. He says I'm good (26) _____ to join a club and swim in a team. What's yours like? (27) _____ you enjoy it? Is it expensive to join?

New Message

From: Tania
To: Jason

My club is great! We're practising tomorrow, so (28) _____ don't you come and meet everyone? (29) _____ you decide you like it, you can join immediately. It's not expensive (30) _____ don't worry about the cost.

TIP STRIP

Question 25: Which word do you put in front of a superlative adjective?

Question 26: The missing word means 'the necessary amount'.

Question 27: You need a question word here, and notice that it is the present simple tense.

Question 28: You need a question word that will complete a phrase we use when making a suggestion.

Question 29: Which word do we use to join two ideas, when one will only happen if the other is true?

Question 30: You need a word to introduce a result.

Part 6

Question 31

Your English friend Chris was ill and hasn't got the information about the school trip. Write an email to Chris.

Tell Chris:
- **when** the school trip is happening
- **where** you are going
- **how much** it costs.

Write **25 words** or more.

TIP STRIP

Begin your email with *Dear Chris* or *Hi Chris*.

End with *From, Best wishes* or *See you soon*, and your name.

Remember to include information about all three of the points.

Part 7

Question 32

Look at the three pictures.

Write the story shown in the pictures.

Write **35 words** or more.

TIP STRIP

Look carefully at the pictures. Think about what is happening in each one. Who are the people? What are they doing? Why?

Think about the order of the events/actions in the story. Use words like *then*, and *after that* to link them.

Part 1 (about 30 mins)

Questions 1 – 6

For each question, choose the correct answer.

1 What will the weather be like tomorrow?

A B C

2 Where are the boys going to meet their friend Dave?

  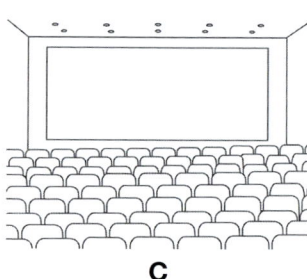
A B C

3 Which birthday card does Nicole choose?

A B C

TIP STRIP

You will hear each recording twice, so don't worry if you are not sure of the answer after the first listening.

Question 1: Look carefully at the pictures. You hear something about each one. Which picture shows today's weather? What does the man say about rain? What did the woman hear on the radio?

Question 2: How do you know they will not meet at the cinema? How many people are going to the burger place?

Question 3: There are two things Nicole does not want on her card. What are they? What does 'countryside' mean? Which card shows this?

4 What did the woman repair?

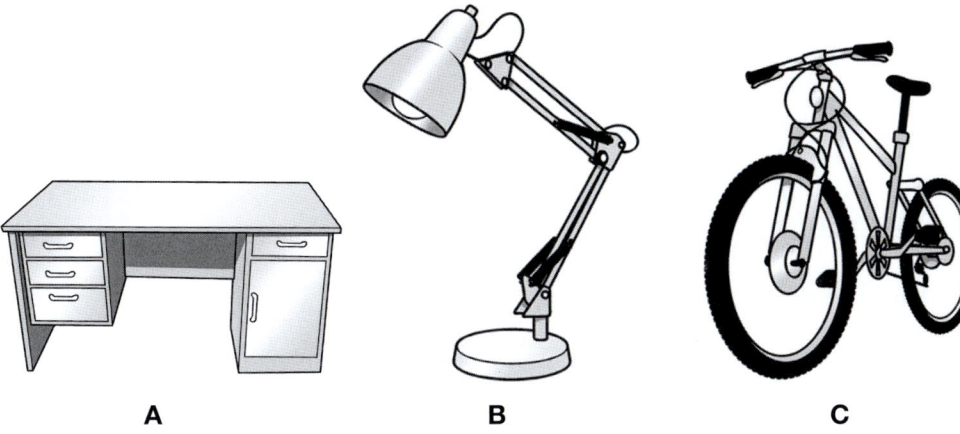

A   B   C

5 Where will they stay when they are on holiday?

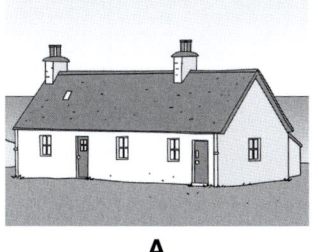  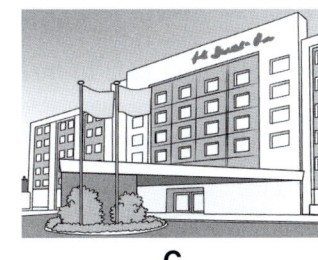

A   B   C

TIP STRIP

Question 4: Be careful! The woman uses the word 'repair' when talking about the lamp. But what does she say? Did she repair it?

Question 5: What's the problem with camping? And what does the man say about hotels? Which idea does he like best?

Part 2

Questions 6 – 10

For each question, write the correct answer in the gap. Write **one word** or **a number** or **a date** or **a time**.

You will hear a woman leaving a message for a friend about a trip to the theatre.

<u>Theatre trip</u>

Name of show: Forest

Day: (6) ....

Price of my ticket: (7) £ ....

Travel by: (8) ....

Name of café to meet at: (9) Café ....

Time to meet: (10) .... p.m.

TIP STRIP

Make sure you understand the context before you start listening. What will the recording be about?

Who will the speaker be?

Question 6: You hear two days mentioned, but only one completes the gap correctly.

Question 7: You will hear two prices mentioned here, but only one completes the gap correctly. Write your answer in numbers, not words, as you will be less likely to make a mistake.

Question 8: What words do you know for ways of travelling? *Bus, car, train, bike*? Listen carefully.

Question 9: This question will test your ability to take down a spelling. Practise the English alphabet often.

Question 10: Here you will write a time. Write it in numbers, not words, as you will be less likely to make a mistake.

Part 3

Questions 11 – 15

For each question, choose the correct answer.

You will hear Ruben and his friend Amy talking about their computers.

11   Ruben bought his tablet because
   - **A**   it has free games.
   - **B**   he liked the size.
   - **C**   the camera was good.

12   Ruben plans to sell his tablet
   - **A**   at a local shop.
   - **B**   to his brother.
   - **C**   on the internet.

13   How much does Ruben want for his tablet?
   - **A**   £200.
   - **B**   £300.
   - **C**   £500.

14   What does Amy like most about her laptop?
   - **A**   the speakers
   - **B**   the memory
   - **C**   the screen

15   Ruben and Amy will meet on
   - **A**   Saturday afternoon.
   - **B**   Sunday morning.
   - **C**   Sunday afternoon.

TIP STRIP

Before the recording starts, you will have time to read through the questions. The questions will tell you what you are going to hear and guide you through the conversation.

Question 11: Ruben talks about the size, the camera and games, but which one was his reason for buying the tablet?

Question 12: Ruben says he is going to put an advertisement online. Which option does this match?

Question 13: Ruben says 'I'd like to get around …' Is this a hope for the future or about the past?

Question 14: Amy likes all these things – but which does she say is the best?

Question 15: When is Amy busy? When is she free?

LISTENING **TEST 2**

Part 4

Questions 16 – 20

For each question, choose the correct answer.

16 You will hear two friends talking about a birthday present.
    What kind of present is it?

    A   a ticket

    B   a magazine

    C   a camera

17 You will hear two friends talking about running.
    What does the woman say about running?

    A   It's easy to hurt yourself.

    B   It's the best way to exercise.

    C   It's becoming more popular.

18 You will hear a woman talking about her new job.
    How does she feel about it?

    A   surprised it is so much fun

    B   worried because it's difficult

    C   upset about some of her colleagues

19 You will hear two friends talking.
    What have they just done?

    A   seen a film

    B   had a meal

    C   met a friend

20 You will hear a man talking on the phone.
    What is he doing?

    A   explaining a problem

    B   asking for advice

    C   making an appointment

TIP STRIP

Question 16: Look at the options and then listen carefully to the vocabulary the speakers use. What has 'articles', 'photos', 'pages' and 'competitions'?

Question 17: Look at options **A**, **B** and **C**. All these ideas are in the text, but the woman only says one of them.

Question 18: Listen to what the woman says at the beginning and end of the conversation. Which option does this match?

Question 19: They talk about a friend, but did they see him tonight? They talk about a meal, but have they eaten yet?

Question 20: Listen carefully for why the man is talking. Does he ask for advice? Does he already have an appointment?

Part 5

Questions 21 – 25

For each question, choose the correct answer.

You will hear Rita talking to a friend about her family's hobbies.

What hobby does each person have?

Example:

0   cousin | D |

People

21   sister   [ ]

22   brother   [ ]

23   mum   [ ]

24   dad   [ ]

25   grandad   [ ]

Hobbies

A   acting

B   collecting toys

C   computer games

D   cooking

E   making music

F   photography

G   travelling

H   watching films

TIP STRIP

You will hear the people in the same order as in the listening text. You will hear the exact words e.g. 'sister'. You may hear the options **A – H** as they are written, or you may hear words that mean the same thing. Listen carefully.

Question 21: Which option matches 'going round the world. She's in Thailand at the moment.'

Question 22: You hear something about music and something about video games. Which is the answer?

Question 23: Mum buys old dolls and has lots of them. Which hobby does this match?

Question 24: If someone is in a play, what are they doing?

Question 25: You hear the word 'computer', but what is the correct answer?

TEST 2 SPEAKING

Part 1 (3–4 minutes)

Phase 1

The examiner will ask you and your partner some questions about yourself.
- What's your name?
- How old are you?
- Do you work or are you a student?
- Where do you come from?
- Where do you live?

TIP STRIP

Part 1 Phase 1

My name's …

I'm … years old.

I'm a student/I work in a bank.

I come from …/I'm from … (Which country? How do you say your country in English?)

I live in … (You can say the name of your village, town or city.)

Phase 2

Now, let's talk about **home**

A, how many rooms are there in your home?
Which is your favourite room?

B, where do you eat meals in your home?
What do you like to do in your living room?

Extended response

Now **A**, please tell me something about the people you live with.

Now, let's talk about **reading**.

B, how often do you read a book or a magazine?
What kind of books do you like?

A, where do you like to read?
Where do you get your books and magazines?

Extended response

Now, **B**, please tell me something about your favourite book.

Extra questions
How many people live in your home?
Do you have any brothers or sisters?
Who is the youngest person in your home?

Extra questions
What's your favourite book about?
When did you read the book?
Why do you like it?

TIP STRIP

Part 1 Phase 2
Home

A Say how many and give their names, e.g. kitchen/living room/bathroom/bedrooms.

Say which room and why. Is it comfortable/warm/attractive?

B Say which room. Do you always eat in the same room?

Say the activities. Do you watch TV/listen to music/chat with your family?

Extended response

Say how many and who they are. Your parents/brother(s)/sister(s)/friend(s)?

Also, what are their names? How old are they? Do they work or study?

TIP STRIP

Part 1 Phase 2
Reading

B Say how often, e.g. *every day/in the evenings/once a week/only at the weekends/never*.

Say the kind of books. Do you like books that make you laugh/stories/books about facts?

A Say where. In your room? In bed? At school? On the bus?

Do you borrow them from the library/from friends? Do you get them as presents? Do you buy them in a bookshop?

Extended response

Give the title and say what it is about.

Also, say when you read it and why you like it. Is it interesting/exciting/sad/easy/long/short? Did it teach you something?

Part 2 (5–6 minutes)

Phase 1

The examiner will show you some pictures and ask you and your partner to talk about the things they show.

Now, in this part of the test you are going to talk together.
(Turn to the pictures on page 165.)

Here are some pictures that show different ways of **travelling**.

Do you like these different ways of travelling? Say why or why not. I'll say that again.
Do you like these different ways of travelling? Say why or why not.
All right? Now, talk together.

🕐 about 1–2 minutes

The examiner will ask you at least one question each.

Do you think …

… travelling by train is fast?
… going on a boat is fun?
… sitting in a car is comfortable?
… riding a bicycle is good for you?
… using the bus is expensive?

So, **A**, which of these ways of travelling do you like best?
And you, **B**, which of these ways of travelling do you like best?

🕐 about 1–2 minutes

Thank you.

Phase 2

Now, do you prefer travelling alone or with other people, **B**? (Why?)
And what about you, **A**? (Do you prefer travelling alone or with other people?) (Why?)

What new way of travelling would you like to try, **A**? (Why?)
And you, **B**? (What new way of travelling would you like to try?) (Why?)

🕐 maximum 2 minutes

Thank you. That is the end of the test.

TIP STRIP

Part 2 Phase 1

Name the five ways of travelling you can see in the pictures.

Explain why you like or don't like each one. Is it expensive/slow/fast/exciting/boring/healthy?

Say which is your favourite, e.g.
My favourite way of travelling is …/I like travelling by … better than all the others/I think the best way to travel is …

Extra questions
Why?/Why not?
What do you think?

TIP STRIP

Part 2 Phase 2

Try to explain why you prefer travelling alone or with friends. What do you like to do when you travel – talk or listen to music?

Think of another way of travelling that you have never tried, but you would like to. It may not be in the pictures, e.g. flying in a plane or helicopter, or going on a motorbike. Say why.

TEST 3

Part 1

Questions 1 – 6

For each question, choose the correct answer.

1

Why has Sally written this message?

A to ask Jenny what time she is going to the cinema

B to find out if Jenny would like a lift to the cinema

C to suggest that Jenny meets her outside the cinema

2

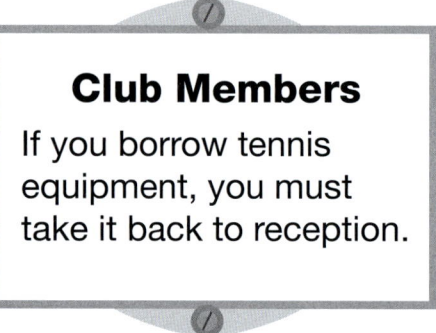

Club Members

If you borrow tennis equipment, you must take it back to reception.

A If you join the club, you must bring your own equipment.

B You should return the club's tennis rackets after using them.

C Members must let reception know when they have finished playing.

3

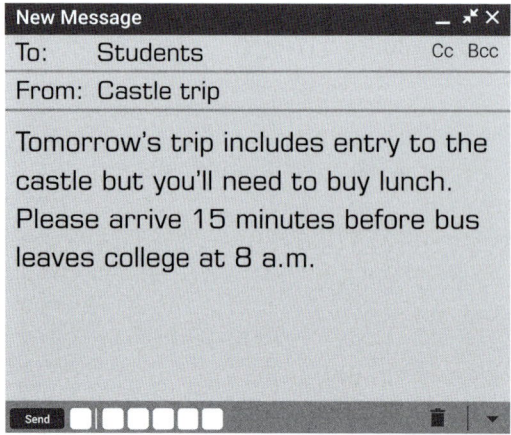

Students going on the castle trip tomorrow will have to

A bring some money with them.

B arrive at college at 8.00 a.m.

C buy a ticket to get into the castle.

4

No swimming class today – Mr Grey's ill.

Next week's lesson is 30 minutes longer.

A The swimming class today will be 30 minutes shorter than usual.

B Everyone should arrive 30 minutes before the swimming class begins.

C It will be possible to swim for an extra 30 minutes in the next class.

5

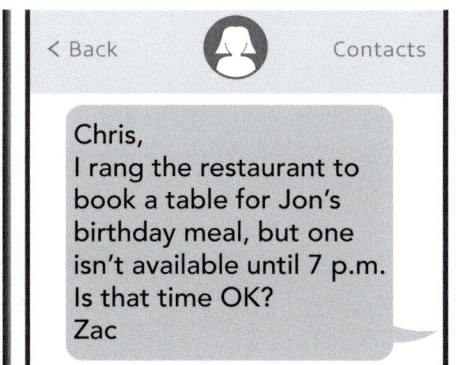

Chris,
I rang the restaurant to book a table for Jon's birthday meal, but one isn't available until 7 p.m. Is that time OK?
Zac

What is Zac doing in this message?

A checking if Chris minds starting a meal at 7 p.m.

B suggesting somewhere to go for a meal

C inviting Chris to a birthday meal

6

City Museum
Visitors must leave all backpacks with staff at front desk.

A You cannot enter the museum until you have bought a ticket.

B Museum staff will need to look inside visitors' bags.

C You are not allowed to take a backpack into the museum.

Part 2

Questions 7 – 13

For each question, choose the correct answer.

		Kamil	Mia	Liam
7	Who says their favourite computer game was a gift?	A	B	C
8	Who often plays computer games with other people?	A	B	C
9	Who has seen a new computer game they would like to buy?	A	B	C
10	Who prefers playing computer games to doing sport?	A	B	C
11	Who has got better at playing their favourite computer game?	A	B	C
12	Who is not allowed to play computer games every day?	A	B	C
13	Who prefers computer games that teach something?	A	B	C

Computer games

Three teenagers talk about playing computer games.

Kamil

I spend about five hours a week playing computer games. My parents don't mind because they know it's less time than some teenagers spend on the computer. I've got all kinds of games, but the ones I like most are those where you learn things. I've got a brilliant game called 'History Ship'. It shows you what life was like on sailing ships hundreds of years ago and it's fun to play. There's another interesting game I'd like to get called 'Space Journey'. It's quite expensive, but I think I'll have enough money for it soon.

Mia

Both of my brothers love being outdoors playing football, but the hobby I enjoy most is playing computer games. My parents are OK with that because they think you can learn a lot from playing games. The only thing they say is that I can't play games on the evenings I have homework. I've got a variety of games, but my favourite is called 'Forestworld'. A friend said it was an amazing game, so I was really pleased when I got it as a present for my birthday.

Liam

I've enjoyed playing computer games for as long as I can remember. I have lots of different games, but the one I like most is called 'Sea Adventure'. It's a really great game. I wasn't very good at it at first, but I've improved and can complete the different levels really quickly now. Several of my friends like computer games too, so they come round to my house at the weekend and we play together. It's great fun!

Part 3

Questions 14 – 18

For each question, choose the correct answer.

A round-the-world trip
Alice Woods and her brother Luke went on a special holiday.

When I was 16, my parents decided to take me and my brother Luke out of school for six months to travel around the world. They wanted us to visit lots of different countries and have new experiences. They said we were old enough to do that kind of trip and believed it was better for us than spending six months in the classroom.

We both had to continue with our studies during the trip, so nearly every day we had online classes in subjects like maths and science. Our parents also made sure we studied the history of the places we visited, and when we had time, we went to museum exhibitions or read guidebooks.

We did some fantastic things on the trip, like sailing along the Mekong River in Vietnam and visiting the Taj Mahal in India. Luke enjoyed travelling around the Amboseli National Park in Kenya. He's interested in wildlife and loved seeing the elephants. I enjoyed that too, but for me the best part was visiting the Rocky Mountains in Canada. We camped there for a few days and the views were amazing!

It was a great trip, but now we're home again, I'm happy to be back at school and spending time with my classmates. Everyone asks if I missed things while I was away – like my favourite food or having my own room – but I tell them not really. It was an adventure and I enjoyed everything about it.

14 Why did Alice's parents decide to take the family on a round-the-world trip?

- **A** They were a little bored with life at home.
- **B** They believed it was a good way to learn new things.
- **C** They wanted to visit other countries while the children were still young.

15 Alice says that most days she and Luke

- **A** visited an exhibition.
- **B** read a guidebook.
- **C** did lessons on the internet.

16 What is Alice doing in the third paragraph?

- **A** explaining how to plan a trip
- **B** describing some activities they did
- **C** giving advice to people who enjoy travelling

17 Which place did Alice enjoy visiting the most?

- **A** the Taj Mahal in India
- **B** the Rocky Mountains in Canada
- **C** the Amboseli National Park in Kenya

18 How does Alice feel now that their trip has finished?

- **A** glad to see her friends again
- **B** happy to eat meals cooked at home
- **C** pleased to be back in her own room

Part 4

Questions 19 – 24

For each question, choose the correct answer.

Life before mobile phones

Today, **(19)**............... all teenagers have a mobile phone and cannot imagine life without one. But most of their parents did not have a mobile phone when they were young – the **(20)**............... of one did not even enter their heads.

Twenty-five years ago, young people did not **(21)**............... to their friends on the phone very much. There were phones in the home, but these were used by the **(22)**............... family. Instead, young people often met up with their friends and did a variety of activities with them.

Today, many parents are happy for their teenage children to have a phone. They think there are good **(23)**............... for them having one. For example, if their children are out, they can call them to **(24)**............... where they are and what time they will be home.

19	A	already	B	nearly	C	easily
20	A	idea	B	thing	C	difference
21	A	say	B	tell	C	speak
22	A	whole	B	full	C	extra
23	A	ways	B	reasons	C	sorts
24	A	look out	B	go out	C	find out

Part 5

Questions 25 – 30

For each question, write the correct answer. Write one word for each gap.

Example: | 0 | for |

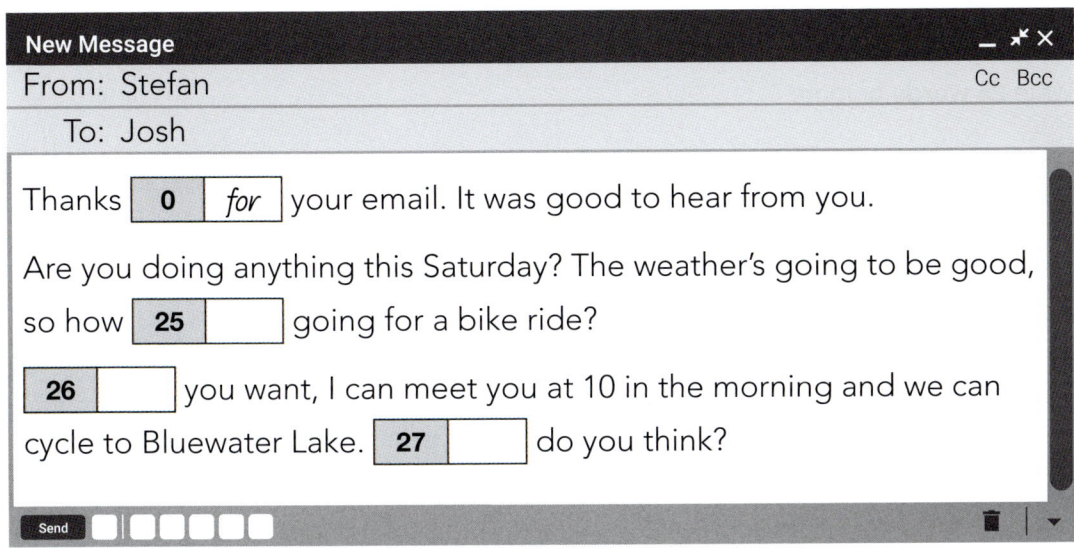

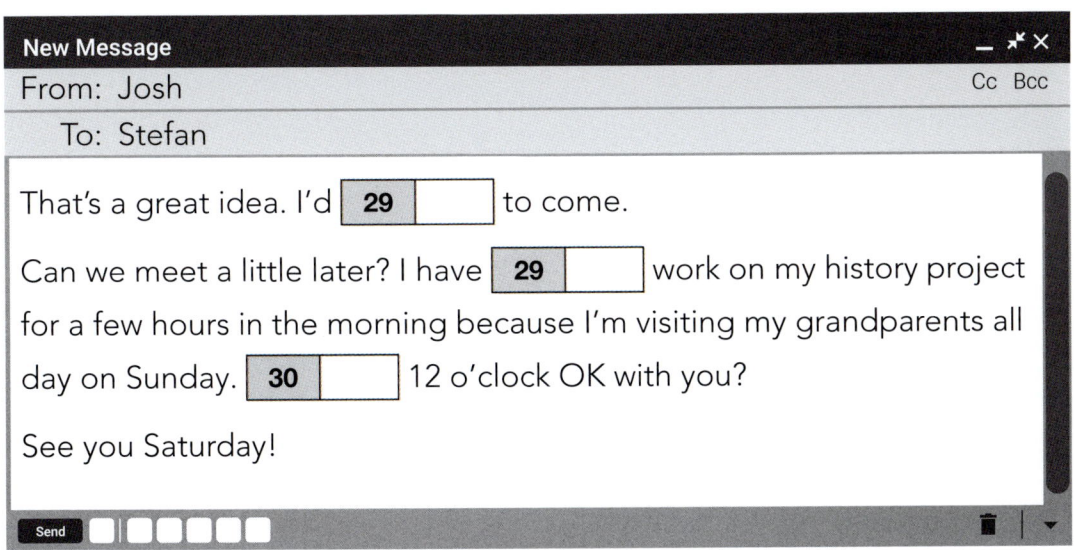

25. about
26. If
27. What
28. love
29. to
30. Is

Part 6

Question 31

Your friend Jo wants to know about your new home. Write an email to Jo.

In your email say:
- **how far** it is from the centre of town
- **which room** is your favourite
- what your **new neighbours** are like.

Write **25 words** or more.

Part 7

Question 32

Look at the three pictures.

Write the story shown in the pictures.

Write **35 words** or more.

Part 1

Questions 1 – 5

For each question, choose the correct answer.

1 What does Lucy decide to buy?

  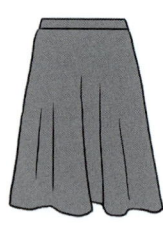

A   B   C

2 What time will they meet at the cinema?

A   B   C

3 Which photo are they looking at?

A   B   C

4 How far will they cycle tomorrow?

A

B

C

5 Where is Anna going on holiday next year?

A

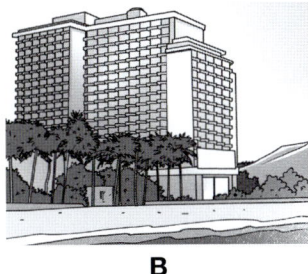
B

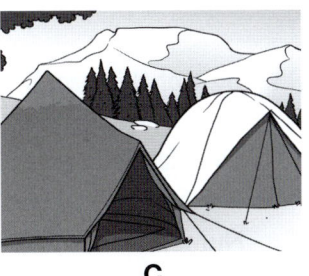
C

Part 2

Questions 6 – 10

For each question, write the correct answer in the gap. Write **one word** or **a number** or **a date** or **a time**.

You will hear some information on the radio about a competition to win tickets for a film festival.

Competition to win film festival tickets

Name of film festival:	Teen Film Festival
Date of this year's festival:	(6) ....
Time festival starts:	(7) .... p.m.
Number to send message to:	(8) ....
What to include in message:	(9) your name, ... and your favourite film
Day you will know if you have won:	(10) ....

Part 3

Questions 11 – 15

For each question, choose the correct answer. You will hear Oliver talking to his friend Noah about a camping trip.

11 Where is the campsite they will visit?
- A in the mountains
- B next to the sea
- C in a forest

12 Why does Oliver think it is a good campsite?
- A It has got a small shop.
- B The people are friendly.
- C You can do activities there.

13 How will they travel to the campsite?
- A by bike
- B by car
- C by bus

14 What does Noah say the weather will be like on Saturday?
- A wet in the morning
- B sunny all day
- C cloudy in the afternoon

15 What does Noah need to bring?
- A some food
- B a tent
- C boots

Part 4

Questions 16 – 20

For each question, choose the correct answer.

16 You will hear a man talking about an art exhibition he went to.

Why did he like the paintings?

- A   They were beautiful.
- B   They were unusual.
- C   They were very old.

17 You will hear a man talking to his friend about his cycling trip.

What was a problem for the man?

- A   He felt very tired.
- B   The weather was bad.
- C   He forgot to pack something to eat.

18 You will hear Alice talking to Chris about a history project they are doing together.

Why can't Chris do the project on Wednesday?

- A   He's going to a concert.
- B   He's playing sport.
- C   He's going to a party.

19 You will hear a teenager talking to her friend about a science competition she took part in. How did she feel about the competition?

- A   excited that she won
- B   happy that she made new friends
- C   pleased that she learnt something new

20 You will hear two friends talking about the volleyball club they belong to.

What does the girl like most about the club?

- A   the club coach
- B   the place the club meets
- C   the people who belong to the club

Part 5

Questions 21 – 25

For each question, choose the correct answer.

You will hear a boy talking to a friend about the activities their classmates are doing on Saturday. What activity is each person doing on Saturday?

Example:

0   Leo   **E**

Classmates

21   Emma

22   Ben

23   Sophie

24   Helen

25   Tim

Activities

A   doing homework

B   going cycling

C   going shopping

D   playing computer games

E   practising piano

F   preparing a meal

G   visiting a family member

H   watching television

LISTENING **TEST 3**

TEST 3 SPEAKING

Part 1 (3–4 minutes)

Phase 1

The examiner will ask you and your partner some questions about yourself.
- What's your name?
- How old are you?
- Do you work or are you a student?
- Where do you come from?
- Where do you live?

Phase 2

Now, let's talk about **watching TV**.

A, how often do you watch TV?
Who do you like watching TV with?

B, when did you last watch TV?
Do you watch sport on TV?

Extended response

Now **A**, please tell me something about your favourite television programme.

Extra questions
What is your favourite programme about?
Which day is your favourite programme on TV?
Do you watch your favourite programme with your family?

Now, let's talk about **studying**.

B, how many hours do you study each day?
Do you like studying?

A, do you study at home in the evening?
Do you like studying alone or with other people?

Extended response

Now **B**, please tell me something about the subjects you enjoy studying.

Extra questions
Which subject do you enjoy studying the most?
Do you prefer doing sport to studying?
Which subject do you not like studying?

Part 2 (5–6 minutes)

Phase 1

The examiner will show you some pictures and ask you and your partner to talk about the things they show.

Now, in this part of the test you are going to talk together.
(Turn to the pictures on page 166.)

Here are some pictures that show different **places in a city.**

Do you like visiting these different places? Say why or why not. I'll say that again.
Do you like visiting these different places? Say why or why not.
All right? Now, talk together.

⏲ about 1–2 minutes

The examiner will ask you at least one question each.

Do you think

… watching football at a stadium is exciting?
… shopping in a market is cheap?
… castles are interesting?
… going to a park is nice?
… going to a museum is boring?

Extra questions
Why?/Why not?
What do you think?

So, **A**, which of these places in the city do you like visiting the most?

And you, **B**, which of these places in the city do you like visiting the most?

⏲ about 1–2 minutes

Thank you.

Phase 2

Now, do you prefer visiting places with family or with friends, **B**? (Why?)

And what about you, **A**? (Do you prefer visiting places with friends or with family?) (Why?)

Do you prefer spending time in a city or the countryside, **A**? (Why?)

And you, **B**? (Do you prefer spending time in a city or the countryside?) (Why?)

⏲ maximum 2 minutes

Thank you. That is the end of the test.

TEST 4

Part 1

Questions 1 – 6

For each question, choose the correct answer.

1

Climbing Centre

Open Tuesday–Sunday

Bring comfortable sports clothes – climbing shoes available at centre

A   You will need to bring special shoes to wear.

B   You can do this activity on any day of the week.

C   You should take the right kind of clothes with you.

2

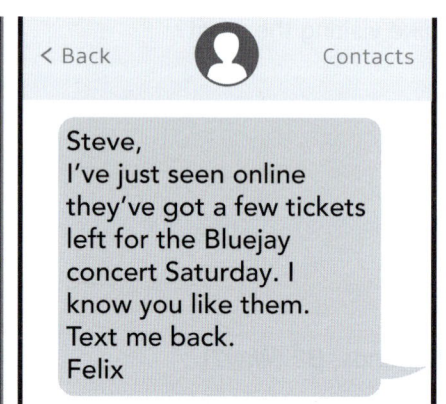

Why has Felix written this message?

A   to find out if Steve is interested in going to a concert

B   to tell Steve that no more tickets are available for a concert

C   to suggest to Steve that they go to a different concert on Saturday

3

A   You have to be quick if you want to buy a cheap computer game.

B   All the computer games in this store are new titles.

C   Some computer games are half-price in the sale

4

New Message
To: Students
From: Mr Garside

You can do your geography project in pairs — but you have to agree on the topic. You must finish it by Friday.

A Students need to decide on their project topic by Friday.

B Students are allowed to work on their projects with a classmate.

C Students should talk to the teacher for advice about their project.

5

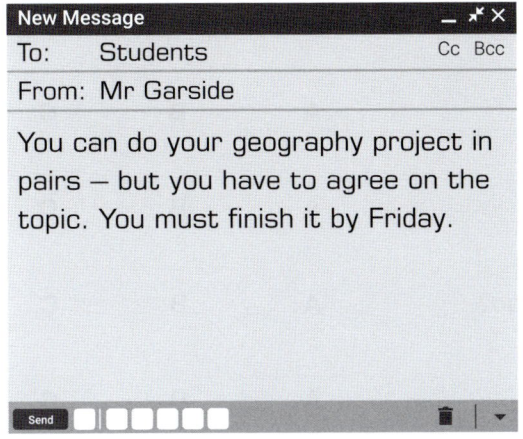

Interested in learning to cook food from around the world?

Go to Room 4C Friday 7 p.m. Everyone welcome — you do not need to bring anything.

A You need experience of cooking to join this class.

B You must bring with you the food you'll need for cooking a meal.

C You should go here if you'd like to cook a variety of dishes.

6

Jess,

Your volleyball coach rang. Practice has changed from Friday to Thursday evening (the same time). Can you go then? He wants to know.

Carla

A The coach wants Jess to know there will be practice twice a week now.

B Jess should contact the coach to tell him if she's available on Thursday evening.

C The coach is telling Jess to stop being late for basketball practice.

READING AND WRITING **TEST 4**   83

Part 2

Questions 7 – 13

For each question, choose the correct answer.

		Becky	Dom	Josie
7	Who travels a long way to a pool?	A	B	C
8	Who has come first in a swimming race?	A	B	C
9	Who does swimming practice daily?	A	B	C
10	Who writes online about swimming?	A	B	C
11	Who swims faster now than 12 months ago?	A	B	C
12	Who does various sports?	A	B	C
13	Who swims at the same club as a family member?	A	B	C

Swimming

Three teenagers talk about their sport.

Becky

I've always loved swimming and a few years ago, I joined a swimming club with my older brother. Our mum drives us to the local pool every morning. It's not far in the car, but practice starts at 6 a.m., so we have to get up early. My brother does other sports and is fitter than me, but I'm hoping to improve and get faster. Maybe one day, I'll even win a competition!

Dom

My mum took me to the pool a lot when I was very young and I've belonged to a swimming club since I was about seven. I now swim for three hours every day except Monday. I need to stay fit, so I run and go to the gym as well. I've always been a fast swimmer and I'm lucky enough to have won a few competitions. I'd like other teenagers to do more sport, so I've started a blog about swimming and staying healthy.

Josie

I had to change my swimming club about a year ago because my family moved house. I like my new club, but the coach makes us work hard. In many ways, that's a good thing. I'm much fitter and my swim times have improved – for example, I can swim a length of the pool more quickly now. Unfortunately, our new house isn't close to the pool and it takes about an hour to get there. I'm sometimes glad when it's the weekend and I can stay at home!

Part 3

Questions 14 – 18

For each question, choose the correct answer.

My fashion blog

17-year-old Jayden Spahn talks about her love of fashion.

I've loved clothes since I was about five. Each morning, I spend time thinking about what to wear. My mum gets angry sometimes and tells me to hurry up, but I don't think it's something you can decide quickly. It's far too important.

Last year, after reading a fashion blog by Rachel, a 19-year-old student, I decided to start one myself. Almost immediately, I posted my first blog. I was really pleased when friends said they loved it – they especially liked the video I made called *A world of fashion*.

I post something new each day. I keep a fashion diary, where I describe what I'm wearing, and every week I also post a photo of myself in my favourite clothes. Most people say they like the photos. But, for me, the best part is getting messages from fans.

My parents think it's good for me to have a hobby, and I still do all my homework, so they're happy for me to do the blog. The only thing they tell me is to be careful about what I read online. They tell me not to worry if people post things that I don't agree with.

I'm not really interested in becoming a fashion model – I think I might get bored with someone taking my photograph every day! Maybe, when I'm older, I'll start my own clothes company, but before that I'm going to do a fashion course at college. I'm already trying to choose the best one!

14 What do we learn about Jayden in the first paragraph?

- **A** She gets her love of fashion from her mother.
- **B** She chooses carefully which clothes to put on.
- **C** She has many clothes she likes wearing to school.

15 Jayden began her fashion blog after

- **A** she watched a video of a fashion show.
- **B** she talked to her friends about starting one.
- **C** she read a blog written by another teenager.

16 What does Jayden enjoy most about her fashion blog?

- **A** posting photos of herself
- **B** writing things in her fashion diary
- **C** receiving messages from her fans

17 How do Jayden's parents feel about her doing a fashion blog?

- **A** pleased she is doing something she enjoys
- **B** worried she will spend less time doing college work
- **C** glad she is sharing her ideas with other young people

18 What has Jayden decided to do in the future?

- **A** start her own company
- **B** work as a fashion model
- **C** study fashion at college

Part 4

Questions 19 – 24

For each question, choose the correct answer.

The Galapagos Islands

The Galapagos Islands are in the Pacific Ocean, about 1000 km off the coast of Ecuador. There are thirteen main islands and seven smaller islands, as **(19)**............ as a number of large rocks. The largest island, which is called Isabella, is 4670 square km.

The islands are famous for their wide **(20)**............ of plants and animals. The nineteenth-century British scientist Charles Darwin visited several of the islands and **(21)**............ the many different animals and plants he saw there.

Today, over 30 percent of the plants and animals on the Galapagos Islands cannot be found anywhere else in the world, so many people who are **(22)**............ in nature visit the islands. **(23)**............, it is important that the islands are **(24)**............ safe for the many animals that live there.

19	A	soon	B	well	C	much
20	A	kind	B	sort	C	variety
21	A	learnt	B	studied	C	looked
22	A	special	B	interested	C	pleasant
23	A	However	B	Actually	C	Unfortunately
24	A	put	B	kept	C	taken

Part 5

Questions 25 – 30

For each question, write the correct answer. Write one word for each gap.

Example: | 0 | for |

New Message
From: Rafael
To: Thomas

Thanks | 0 | for | for agreeing to be my online friend. Let | 25 | tell you a bit about myself.

My name is Rafael and I'm 16 years old. I live in Madrid | 26 | my parents and my brother Xavier, who is two years older | 27 | I am. I go to | 28 | same school as my brother. We walk there together | 29 | day. I like school and have lots of friends there.

My hobby is football and I'm a Real Madrid fan. If I can get a ticket, I go to the Bernabéu stadium to watch them play. How about you? | 30 | you got any hobbies?

Part 6

Question 31

You want to go for a picnic on Saturday with your English friend, Alex.

Write an email to Alex.
___

In your email:

- **ask** Alex **to go for a picnic with you** on Saturday
- **say where** you want to go for a picnic
- **tell** Alex **what to bring**.

Write **25 words** or more.

Part 7

Question 32

Look at the three pictures.

Write the story shown in the pictures.

Write **35 words** or more.

Part 1

Questions 1 – 5

For each question, choose the correct answer.

1 What is Zac doing at the moment?

2 What time will Sam leave home?

3 Which animal did Jack see on his holiday?

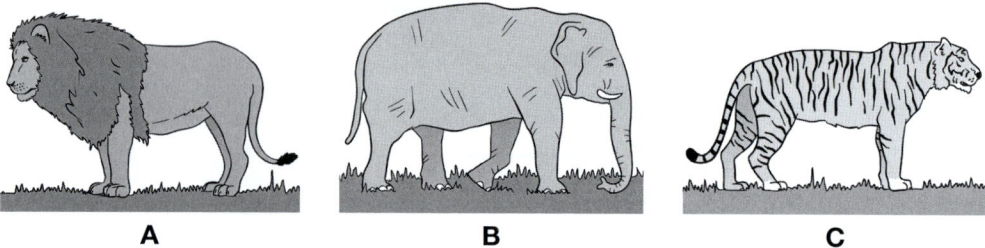

4 What will the weather be like tomorrow?

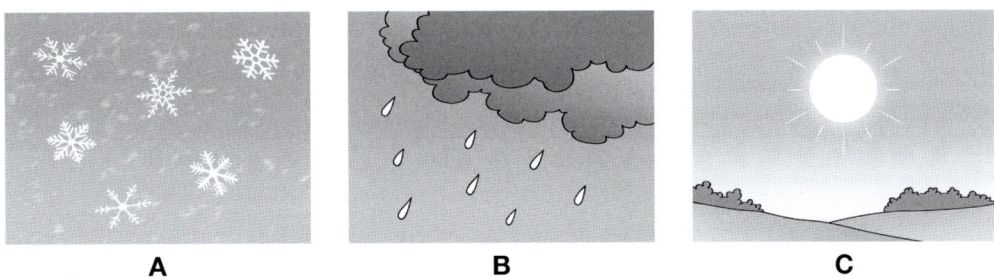

A B C

5 What will Cara eat in the café?

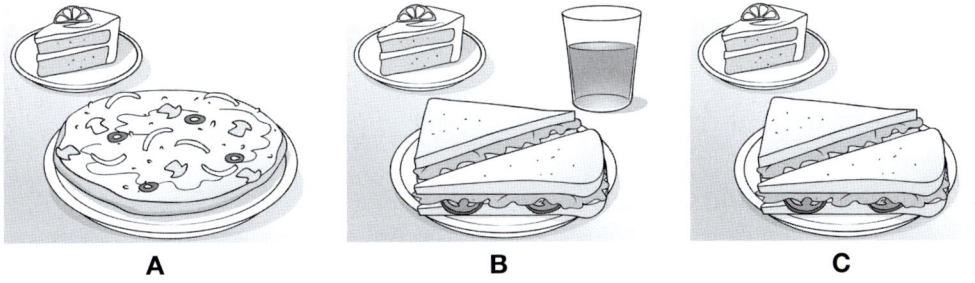

A B C

Part 2

Questions 6 – 10

For each question, write the correct answer in the gap. Write **one word** or **a number** or **a date** or **a time**.

You will hear a teacher talking to a group of students about a trip to a science museum. Listen and complete each question. You will hear the information twice.

Trip to Science Museum

Day of trip:	Thursday
Time to arrive at college:	(6) .... a.m.
Number of students in each group:	(7) ....
Name of most important exhibition:	(8) ....
What to take:	(9) ....
Total cost of trip:	(10) £ ....

Part 3

Questions 11 – 15

For each question, choose the correct answer.

You will hear Amy and her friend Daniel talking about going to the cinema.

11 Which day did Amy go to the cinema with her cousin?

    A   Friday

    B   Saturday

    C   Sunday

12 What time did Amy and her cousin arrive at the cinema?

    A   6.15

    B   6.30

    C   6.45

13 How much did Amy's cinema ticket cost?

    A   £8.00

    B   £10.00

    C   £10.50

14 What did Daniel enjoy least about the last film he saw?

    A   the actors

    B   the music

    C   the story

15 What does Daniel say about the restaurant he went to after the cinema?

    A   His order took a long time.

    B   The food was delicious.

    C   Everything was expensive.

Part 4

Questions 16 – 20

For each question, choose the correct answer.

16 You will hear Ben talking to his friend about his holiday.

What does Ben still need to pack for his holiday?

- A   some winter clothes
- B   a good book
- C   ski equipment

17 You will hear Lisa telling a friend what she did after college yesterday.

What did Lisa do first?

- A   She cooked dinner.
- B   She watched television.
- C   She did a college project.

18 You will hear David talking to a friend about running.

What's David's favourite time of day to go running?

- A   in the morning
- B   at midday
- C   in the evening

19 You will hear Sara talking to a friend about starting university.

What's Sara going to do in the year before she starts university?

- A   get a job
- B   read lots of books
- C   travel around the world

20 You will hear Jack talking to a friend about playing the guitar.

What advice does Jack give his friend?

- A   find a teacher
- B   practise every day
- C   get a music book for beginners

Part 5

Questions 21 – 25

For each question, choose the correct answer.

You will hear Tess talking to a friend about the things her family enjoy reading. What does each person enjoy reading?

Example:

0   Sister | D |

People

21   Mum | |
22   Brother | |
23   Dad | |
24   Grandma | |
25   Cousin | |

Things they enjoy reading

A   adverts
B   blogs
C   books
D   comics
E   emails
F   magazines
G   newspapers
H   text messages

TEST 4

SPEAKING

Part 1 (3–4 minutes)

Phase 1

The examiner will ask you and your partner some questions about yourself.
- What's your name?
- How old are you?
- Do you work or are you a student?
- Where do you come from?
- Where do you live?

Phase 2

Now, let's talk about **music**.

A, do you like listening to music?
How often do you listen to music?

B, where do you listen to music?
Do you like going to concerts with friends?

Extended response

Now **A**, please tell me something about your favourite music.

Extra questions
Do you and your friends like listening to the same kinds of music?
What's your favourite band called?
Why do you like this band?

Now, let's talk about **holidays**.

B, how often do you go on holiday?
What do you like best about going on holiday?

A, what do you like doing when you are on holiday?
Who do you go on holiday with?

Extended response

Now **B**, please tell me something about the last holiday that you went on.

Extra questions
Where did you go for your last holiday?
What was the weather like on your last holiday?
How did you feel after your last holiday?

Part 2 (5–6 minutes)

Phase 1

The examiner will show you some pictures and ask you and your partner to talk about the things they show.

Now, in this part of the test you are going to talk together.
(Turn to the pictures on page 167.)

Here are some pictures that show different **activities.**

Do you like doing these different activities? Say why or why not. I'll say that again.
Do you like doing these different activities? Say why or why not.
All right? Now, talk together.

⏱ about 1–2 minutes

The examiner will ask you at least one question each.

Do you think …

… skateboarding is fun?
… cooking is difficult?
… chess is exciting?
… reading is boring?
… playing computer games is a good idea?

Extra questions
Why?/Why not?
What do you think?

So, **A**, which of these activities do you like best?
And you, **B**, which of these activities do you like best?

⏱ about 1–2 minutes

Thank you.

Phase 2

Now, do you prefer doing activities alone or with other people, **B**? (Why?)
And what about you, **A**? (Do you prefer doing activities alone or with other people?) (Why?)

Which is more fun, doing activities indoors or outdoors, **A**? (Why?)
And you, **B**? (Which is more fun, doing activities indoors or outdoors?) (Why?)

⏱ maximum 2 minutes

Thank you. That is the end of the test.

TEST 5

Part 1

Questions 1 – 5

For each question, choose the correct answer.

1

London–Brighton

Buses every hour
from 07.00 until 22.00
[Mon–Sat]

A There are no buses after 10 p.m. on Tuesdays.

B There is a bus at 8 o'clock on Sunday.

C There are only seven buses a day to Brighton.

2

SCIENCE MUSEUM

£5.50 (under-16-year-olds £3)
Online tickets half price

A Children under three are not allowed in the museum.

B 16-year-olds pay the same as adults.

C It's cheaper to buy your tickets at the museum.

3

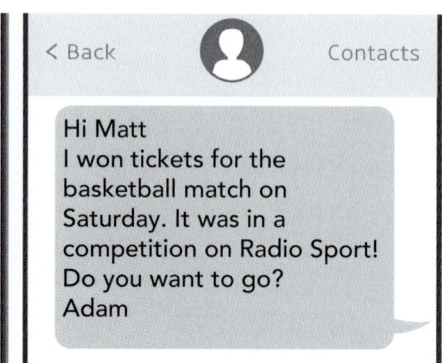

Hi Matt
I won tickets for the basketball match on Saturday. It was in a competition on Radio Sport! Do you want to go?
Adam

A Adam wants to tell Matt about a competition on the radio.

B Adam is inviting Matt to a basketball match.

C Adam has bought Matt tickets to a basketball match.

TEST 5 READING AND WRITING

4

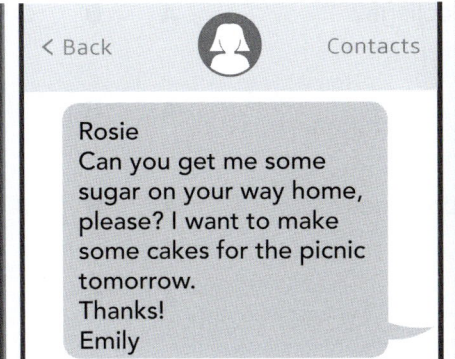

Emily would like Rosie to

A help her make some cakes.

B go to a picnic tomorrow.

C buy some food for her.

5

A Students pay less for the room.

B You can rent the whole house.

C Anyone can rent the room now.

6

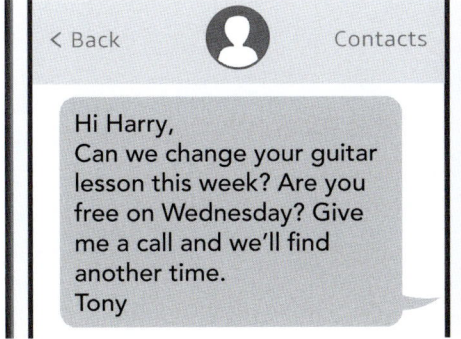

What should Harry do?

A Write an email to Tony.

B Speak to Tony.

C See Tony on Wednesday.

Part 2

Questions 7 – 13

For each question, choose the correct answer.

		Chloë	Ian	Ben
7	Who does their hobby with a family member?	A	B	C
8	Who began to be interested in their hobby at college?	A	B	C
9	Who won a prize for their hobby?	A	B	C
10	Who would like to do their hobby in different countries?	A	B	C
11	Who often spends money on their hobby?	A	B	C
12	Who is planning to buy some expensive equipment for their hobby?	A	B	C
13	Who had help with their hobby from a friend?	A	B	C

What's your hobby?

Chloë

My love of windsurfing started when I was a child. It's quite an expensive hobby for most people, but I'm lucky because my uncle owns a windsurfing school. I can go windsurfing for free with my cousins. They've won prizes for windsurfing in different countries. I'm getting better at windsurfing now. Next year, I'd like to buy my own board. I need to save a lot of money first though!

Ian

I love art. My grandfather was an artist so maybe it's in the family! Unfortunately, I never met him, but I've seen his pictures. My love for art started at college. I don't go to college now, but I go to an art class with my friend. I won't win any prizes for my art – I'm not that good, but I enjoy it. I also love art shops. I probably buy too much – I usually buy something every week!

Ben

My hobby is music. I'm really lucky because my friend's a drum teacher. She's taught me a lot. I now play the drums in a group. I only joined the group last year, but we've already played five concerts – two were at a local college. We entered a music competition last month and won £500! I've always loved music and my dream is to play in different cities around the world.

Part 3

Questions 14 – 18

For each question, choose the correct answer.

My Love for Photography
By Eliza Brinkman

How did I get interested in photography? People usually think it's because of my uncle, the famous photographer Oliver Brinkman. Maybe you've seen his TV show, *Pictures of the World*. However, I started taking photos on a school trip. I remember my grandma lent me her camera.

When I was 16, I studied photography at college. I remember feeling really worried about the course. I loved taking photos but I wasn't sure how good I was. And sometimes it's difficult having a famous uncle. People think you'll be amazing too!

My first job was at the local newspaper. My neighbour heard that the newspaper was looking for a photographer and suggested it to me. My mum said I should try and get the job and I got it! When I arrived for my first day, I found out that an old school friend was also working there.

After five years at the newspaper, I moved to London and started a job at the fashion magazine *Dream*. I loved this job. I worked in a great team; I'll always remember how kind they were to me. I went to very interesting places and worked with some famous models.

I now have my own company, ABC Photography. I have a team of photographers who take photos for different magazines. My newest project is a photography course that I've started at my company. I really want to use my experience in the photography business to help new photographers. It's very exciting!

14 Eliza first became interested in photography when

    A   she saw her uncle's photographs.

    B   she borrowed her grandma's camera.

    C   she watched a TV programme about photography.

15 When Eliza started college she felt …

    A   worried that she was not good enough.

    B   excited about studying photography.

    C   lucky that she knew a famous photographer.

16 Who told Eliza about the job at the newspaper?

    A   an old friend from school

    B   her mum

    C   someone who lived near her

17 What will Eliza never forget about *Dream* magazine?

    A   her colleagues

    B   the places she visited

    C   the famous models

18 Eliza is teaching photography at her company because

    A   she thinks her team needs more training.

    B   she hopes to make more money.

    C   she wants to share what she has learnt.

Part 4

Questions 19 – 24

For each question, choose the correct answer.

Nettie Polano

Nettie Polano is an unusual university student. So what makes her **(19)**............... from other university students? Nettie is amazing – she started university when she was 14! Nettie is a teenage genius – a teenager who is **(20)**............... clever.

She completed primary school in four years and secondary school in only three years! Her teachers saw she was much **(21)**............... than other students her age when she was seven years old. They **(22)**............... Nettie's parents how brilliant she was.

Two years later, Nettie's parents decided to take her out of school. Nettie **(23)**............... her school studies at home with teachers who came to her house. Nettie studies science at university. She chose this **(24)**............... because she dreams of one day becoming the youngest person to travel into space.

19	A	strange	B	different	C	alone
20	A	especially	B	immediately	C	exactly
21	A	older	B	bigger	C	better
22	A	spoke	B	told	C	said
23	A	finished	B	made	C	took
24	A	level	B	term	C	subject

Part 5

Questions 25 – 30

For each question, write the correct answer. Write one word for each gap.

Example: | 0 | at |

New Message

From:
To:

Dear Jack,

I'm sitting on the beach | 0 | at | the moment. I've just | 25 | swimming and soon I'm going to play beach volleyball with my sister and some friends.

We're | 26 | a wonderful time. It's beautiful here. The water is a little cold | 27 | it doesn't matter because it's so hot outside.

We've visited some really interesting places and tomorrow we're going to spend | 28 | whole day walking in the mountains. I've taken lots | 29 | photographs. I'll show you them | 30 | I see you.

We'll be back next week. I'll call you then.

Love,

Kim

Part 6

Question 31

You have lost your mobile phone. You want your English friend, Sam, to help you find it. Write an email to Sam.

In your email:
- tell Sam **where** you lost your mobile phone
- say **why** your mobile phone is important
- **ask** Sam to **help** you find it.

Write **25 words** or more.

Part 7

Question 32

Look at the three pictures.

Write the story shown in the pictures.

Write **35 words** or more.

Part 1

Questions 1 – 5

For each question, choose the correct answer.

1   How much will the woman pay for the laptop?

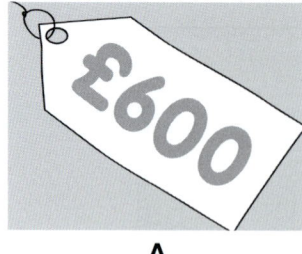   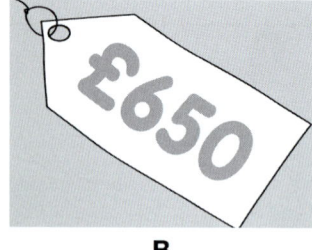   

   A   B   C

2   What's Sue doing now?

   A   B   C

3   What has Tom just finished doing?

   A   B   C

4 Who is Dan meeting at the weekend?

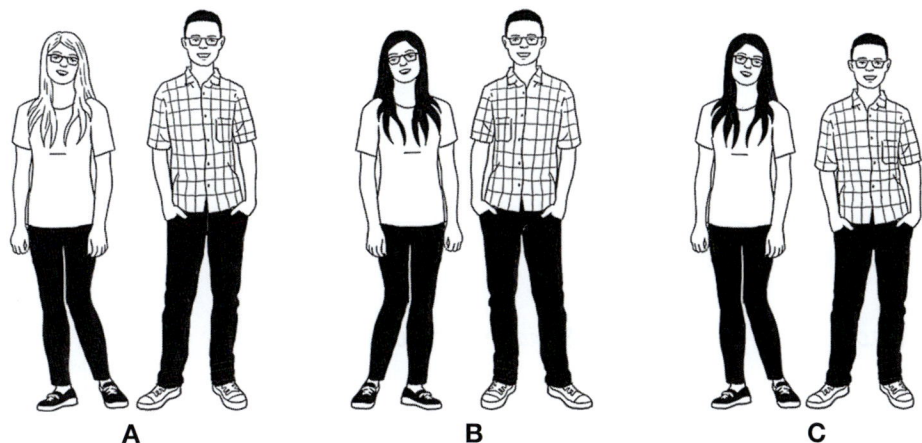

5 What present is the boy going to give Tina?

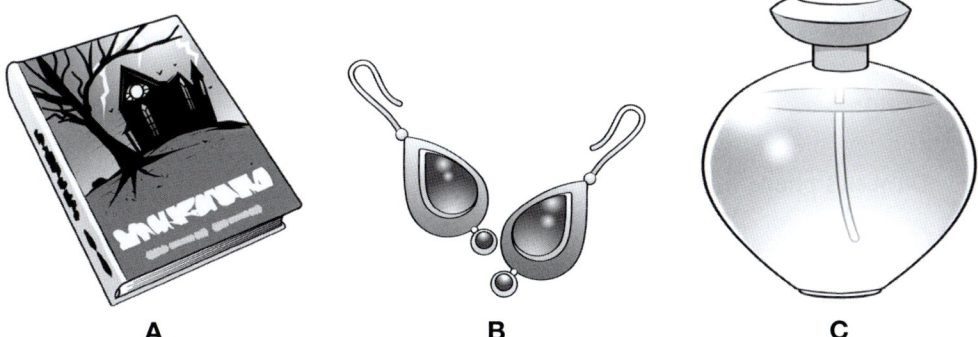

Part 2

Questions 6 – 10

For each question, write the correct answer in the gap. Write **one word** or **a number** or **a date** or **a time**.

You will hear Damien telling his friend about Anna's surprise party.

Anna's surprise party

Place: <u>Banana</u> Restaurant

Time: (6) .... p.m.

Address: (7) 62 .... Street

Travel by: (8) ....

Bring: (9) ....

Damien's phone number: (10) ....

Part 3

Questions 11 – 15

For each question, choose the correct answer.

You will hear Vivienne talking to her brother, Andy, about buying a new video game.

11 What was Vivienne doing when Andy came home?

    A   playing a video game

    B   shopping online

    C   eating

12 What's the name of Vivienne's new video game?

    A   Race Week

    B   Winner

    C   Star Driver

13 Vivienne bought the video game because

    A   she saw it on a TV show.

    B   her friend said it was good.

    C   she heard an advert for it on the radio.

14 Why does Vivienne prefer the shop Small World to Top Computers?

    A   there are more things for sale

    B   the prices are better

    C   the staff are friendlier

15 Andy says the shop Small World was

    A   very crowded.

    B   too noisy.

    C   not very light.

Part 4

Questions 16 – 20

For each question, choose the correct answer.

16   You will hear Jack leaving a message for his friend. What does Jack want his friend to do?

   A   buy some tickets

   B   come to a concert on Saturday

   C   meet Jack's sister after work

17   You will hear a girl, Annabel, talking about her weekend. What does Annabel say about cycling in the mountains?

   A   It's dangerous.

   B   It's hard work.

   C   It's beautiful.

18   You will hear a basketball coach talking to the basketball team. Why must the team do extra practice before the match?

   A   He thinks they can win the match.

   B   The team isn't playing very well.

   C   Some players have missed practice.

19   You will hear a boy, Daniel, talking about a restaurant. What does Daniel say about the restaurant?

   A   The prices should be cheaper.

   B   The meals should be bigger.

   C   The food should be better.

20   You will hear a woman talking to her neighbour about the weather. What was the weather like last night?

   A   It was cold.

   B   It was wet.

   C   It was windy.

Part 5

Questions 21 – 25

For each question, choose the correct answer. You will hear Tim talking to a friend about an activity holiday. What activity did Tim do on each day?

Example:

0   Wednesday | G |

Days

21   Thursday   [ ]

22   Friday   [ ]

23   Saturday   [ ]

24   Sunday   [ ]

25   Monday   [ ]

Activities

A   fishing

B   horse-riding

C   playing board games

D   swimming

E   tennis

F   volleyball

G   walking

H   windsurfing

TEST 5 SPEAKING

Part 1 (3–4 minutes)

Phase 1

The examiner will ask you and your partner some questions about yourself.
- What's your name?
- How old are you?
- Do you work or are you a student?
- Where do you come from?
- Where do you live?

Phase 2

Now, let's talk about **shopping**.

A, when do you like going shopping?
How often do you go shopping for clothes?

B, who do you like going shopping with?
When did you last go shopping?

Extended response

Now **A**, please tell me something about your favourite shop.

Extra questions
Where is your favourite shop?
Why do you like this shop?
What are the shop assistants like?

Now, let's talk about **sport**.

B, what is your favourite sport?
Where can people play sport in your town?

A, who plays the most sport in your family?
What sport did you play when you were younger?

Extended response

Now **B**, please tell me something about the last time you played or watched sport.

Extra questions
What sport did you play/watch?
Who did you play/watch the sport with?
How did you feel when you were playing/watching the sport?

Part 2 (5–6 minutes)

Phase 1

The examiner will show you some pictures and ask you and your partner to talk about the things they show.

Now, in this part of the test you are going to talk together.
(Turn to the pictures on page 168.)

Here are some pictures that show different **places to eat.**

Do you like these different places to eat? Say why or why not. I'll say that again.
Do you like these different places to eat? Say why or why not.

All right? Now, talk together.

🕒 about 1–2 minutes

The examiner will ask you at least one question each.

Do you think …

… picnics are boring?
… eating at home is interesting?
… restaurants are expensive?
… cafés are a good place to eat?
… eating at a market is cheap?

> **Extra questions**
> Why?/Why not?
> What do you think?

So, **A**, which of these places to eat do you like best?
And you, **B**, which of these places to eat do you like best?

🕒 about 1–2 minutes

Thank you.

Phase 2

Now, do you prefer eating outside or inside, **B**? (Why?)
And what about you, **A**? (Do you prefer eating outside or inside?) (Why?)

Which is more fun, cooking for friends or going to a fast food restaurant together, **A**? (Why?)
And you, **B**? (Which is more fun, cooking for friends or going to a fast food restaurant together?) (Why?)

🕒 maximum 2 minutes

Thank you. That is the end of the test.

TEST 6

Part 1

Questions 1 – 6

For each question, choose the correct answer.

1

What should Sarah do?

A   tell Alice if she can join her later

B   meet Alice at the cinema in town

C   invite some friends to the cinema

2

A   Theatre tickets are cheaper online.

B   Students pay less to go to the theatre.

C   Only students can buy these theatre tickets.

3

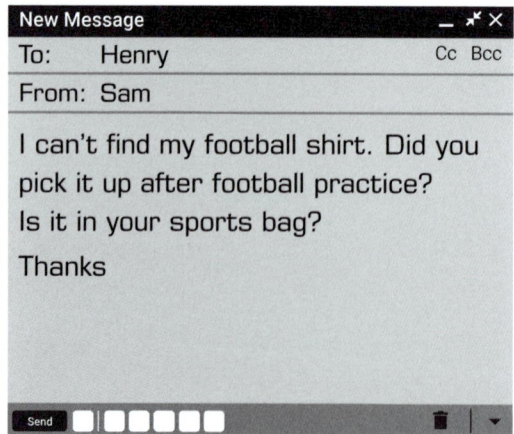

A   Sam has lent Henry his football shirt.

B   Sam's football shirt is in Henry's sports bag.

C   Sam doesn't know where his football shirt is.

4

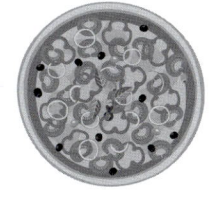

Great offer!

Buy a pizza and get free chips!

Monday–Wednesday only

A Pizzas are cheaper on Mondays and Wednesdays.

B You pay less for pizza and chips from Monday to Wednesday.

C Customers get a free pizza with their chips from Monday to Wednesday.

5

Guitar for sale

Birthday present – never used

£30 cash only

07787 652542

A The guitar is as good as new.

B You can pay by cheque.

C The guitar is a good birthday present.

6

Art Course

Wednesday 7–9

If you're interested email Jo@photo.ac.uk

All levels welcome

A There are 7 to 9 people on each course.

B You can call Jo for more information.

C Beginners can do the course.

Part 2

Questions 7 – 13

For each question, choose the correct answer.

		Louisa	Josh	Anita
7	Who has always lived in London?	A	B	C
8	Who prefers quiet places?	A	B	C
9	Who started a business in London?	A	B	C
10	Who would like to live somewhere else?	A	B	C
11	Who lives in a home with a view?	A	B	C
12	Who likes London in the spring?	A	B	C
13	Who hates their journey to work?	A	B	C

We ♥ London

Louisa

I've lived in London nearly all my life. I love London, but I don't like very crowded, noisy places. I enjoy spending time in the big parks. I love the city in April when they are full of flowers. I have a café in London which I opened two years ago. I travel to work by train. It takes one hour, but I spend the time reading. And I love reading!

Josh

My parents are both from villages, but I was born in London and I've never left. I love being around lots of noise and people. I work for a very successful business in the centre of London. I have a nice apartment – I can see London Bridge from my bedroom window. I'm lucky because I live close to work and it's a pleasant walk from my apartment. I know lots of people hate their journey to work.

Anita

All my family live in London. I went to university in France, but then I came back. London can be very busy and noisy, but I don't mind that. I like big cities. Last spring I went to Tokyo. It was great. My dream is to work there one day. In London, I have a long journey to work and the train is always late. It's the worst part of my day – it's awful! Trains are better in Japan.

Part 3

Questions 14 – 18

For each question, choose the correct answer.

The Greek Waiter

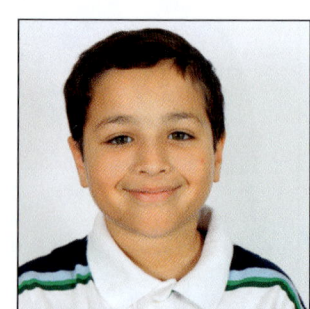

Alexis is ten years old and lives in a small village on a beautiful Greek island. Like all children his age, Alexis has just completed Year 4 in primary school. But Alexis is different from other children his age. He doesn't spend the summer on the beach or playing video games. In the busy summer months Alexis spends his days in his family's restaurant. In July and August, the restaurant is very popular with tourists from all over the world. Because he is the only person in his family who can speak English, it is his job to look after the tourists when they eat at the restaurant. He explains the menu to tourists and takes their orders.

Where did he learn his English? There is no school in Alexis's village, and during the school year he travels 12 kilometres every day by bus to a nearby village to go to school. Together with his classmates, two evenings a week, he attends English classes at a language school in the same village. There is no bus service when his classes end, so his mother picks him up and brings him home. Alexis doesn't mind, he enjoys learning English. He wants to be a journalist so he knows languages will be useful. He is very pleased that he can help his family with their business and the tourists are very happy that they can order their meal in English. He's also learnt a lot about cooking and loves the food at the restaurant!

14 In the summer, Alexis

  A plays video games and goes to the beach.

  B spends July and August on another island.

  C doesn't have a lot of free time.

15 Alexis helps his family in the restaurant because he

  A is a good waiter.

  B likes meeting tourists.

  C can speak English.

16 Where does Alexis go to school?

  A in his village

  B in another village

  C in a nearby town

17 Where does he learn English?

  A in a language school

  B in primary school

  C at home

18 What does Alexis want to do when he's older?

  A write news articles

  B be a language teacher

  C have his own business

Part 4

Questions 19 – 24

For each question, choose the correct answer.

Hip-hop

Hip-hop is more than just a (19)............ of music. For people who love hip hop, it is often a (20)............ of life. The words in the songs are very important as well as how people dance and the how they (21)............ .

Hip-hop started in the Bronx area of New York City in the 1970s. But like all music, hip-hop had its beginnings in (22)............ kind of music. In the case of hip-hop, this music was African-American music, and some even say African music. Since the 1990s hip-hop has (23)............ very popular all over the world. People have enjoyed hip-hop for more than forty years already. Like rock and roll, it will probably (24)............ to be popular for many more years!

19	A	song	B	band	C	type
20	A	fashion	B	way	C	reason
21	A	dress	B	wear	C	show
22	A	another	B	different	C	other
23	A	begun	B	arrived	C	become
24	A	stay	B	continue	C	keep

Part 5

Questions 25 – 30

For each question, write the correct answer. Write one word for each gap.

Example: | 0 | why |

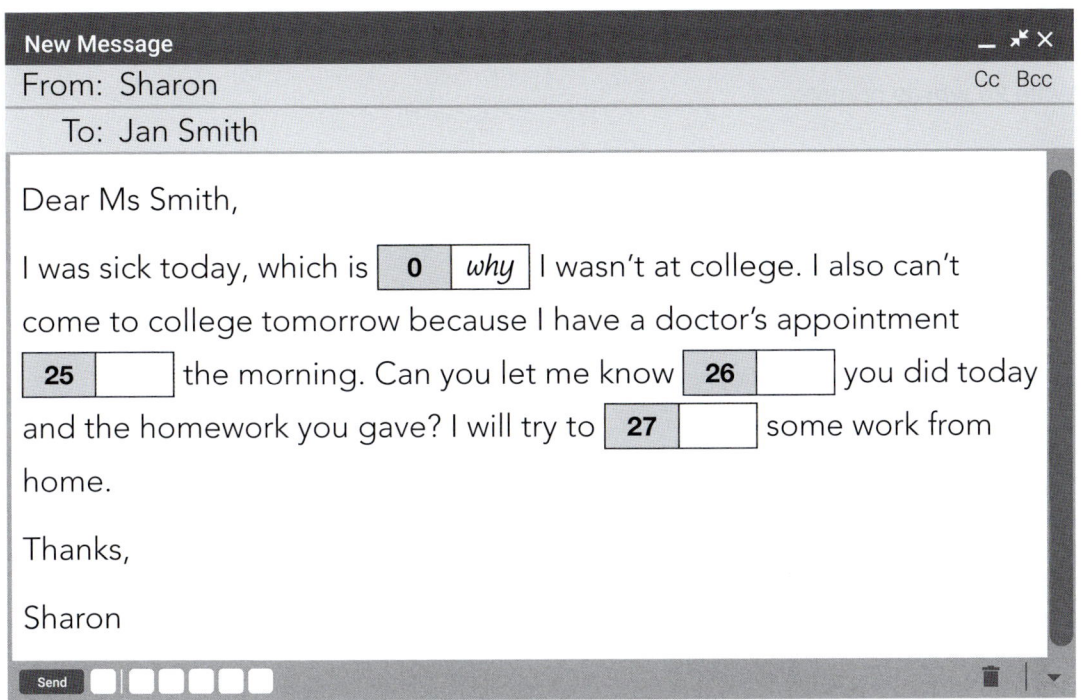

New Message
From: Sharon
To: Jan Smith

Dear Ms Smith,

I was sick today, which is | 0 | why | I wasn't at college. I also can't come to college tomorrow because I have a doctor's appointment | 25 | the morning. Can you let me know | 26 | you did today and the homework you gave? I will try to | 27 | some work from home.

Thanks,

Sharon

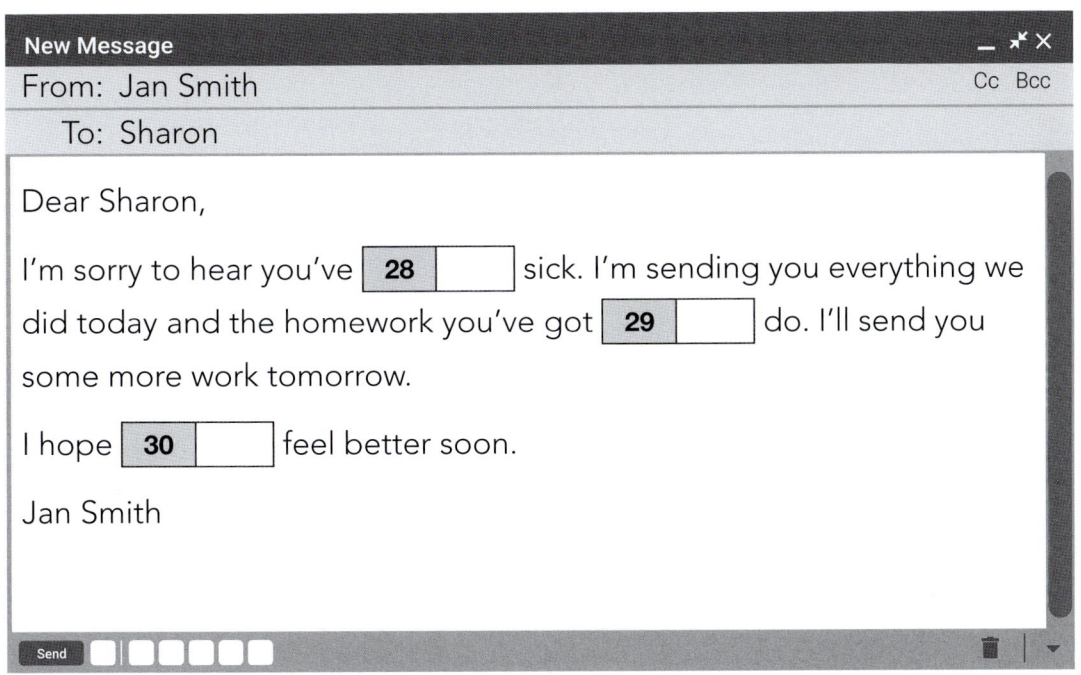

New Message
From: Jan Smith
To: Sharon

Dear Sharon,

I'm sorry to hear you've | 28 | sick. I'm sending you everything we did today and the homework you've got | 29 | do. I'll send you some more work tomorrow.

I hope | 30 | feel better soon.

Jan Smith

Part 6

Question 31

Your friend Toni is coming to visit you next Saturday. Write an email to Toni.

In your email say:
- **what time** you can **meet** Toni
- **where** you can meet
- what you **plan to do together**.

Write **25 words** or more.

Part 7

Question 32

Look at the three pictures.

Write the story shown in the pictures.

Write **35 words** or more.

Part 1

Questions 1 – 5

For each question, choose the correct answer.

1   What was the weather like yesterday?

 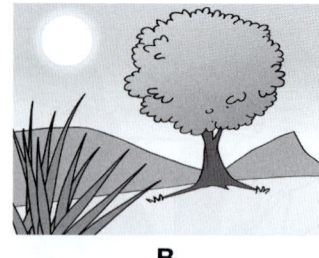 

      A   B   C

2   What has the man left at home?

 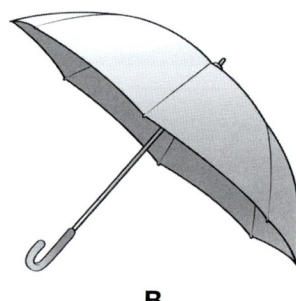 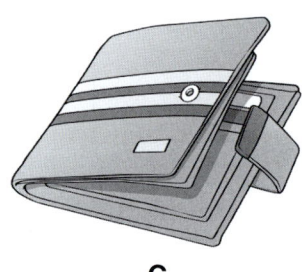

      A   B   C

3   What did the girl cook today?

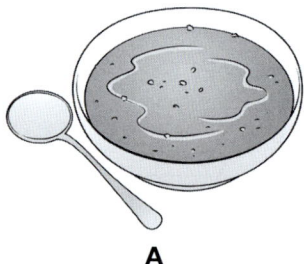  

      A   B   C

4 Which photo are they looking at?

5 What's the new sports centre next to?

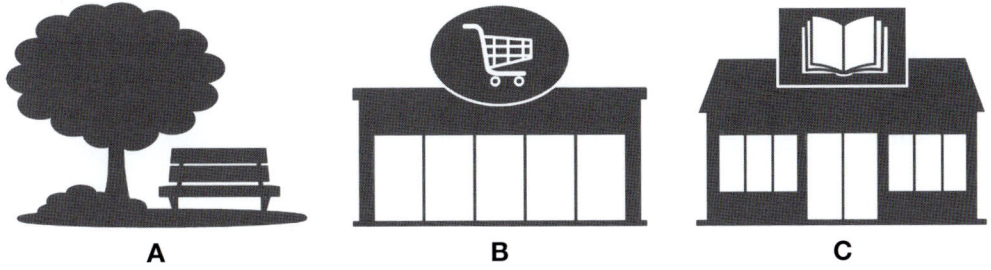

Part 2

Questions 6 – 10

For each question, write the correct answer in the gap. Write **one word** or **a number** or **a date** or **a time**.

You will hear a girl, Antonia, telling her friend about French lessons.

French lessons

Place: <u>Art</u> Centre

Day: (6) ....

Time: (7) .... p.m.

Price per month: (8) £ ....

Teacher: Ms (9) ....

Teacher's phone number: (10) ....

Part 3

Questions 11 – 15

For each question, choose the correct answer. You will hear Nancy talking to her friend, George, about a film she saw.

11 When did Nancy see the film called *The Castle*?
- A   Friday
- B   Saturday
- C   Sunday

12 George thinks *The Castle* is a good film because
- A   he's been to see it at the cinema.
- B   he's heard people talking about it.
- C   he's read about it on the internet.

13 Why did Nancy decide to watch the film?
- A   The story interested her.
- B   She loves horror films.
- C   Her friend wanted to see it.

14 George says that the actor Ed Wesley is
- A   attractive.
- B   funny.
- C   kind.

15 What do George and Nancy both think should change at the new cinema?
- A   the ticket prices
- B   the temperature
- C   the types of films

Part 4

Questions 16 – 20

For each question, choose the correct answer.

16 You will hear two friends talking about a mobile phone. Why didn't the girl buy the phone?

    A   It cost too much.

    B   She bought something more useful.

    C   She needs to save more money.

17 You will hear a sportsman talking on the radio. What advice does he give young people?

    A   Do a sport they enjoy.

    B   Work hard and practise a lot.

    C   Play a new sport for a few weeks.

18 You will hear a woman talking to a friend about a book. Why was she surprised?

    A   She read the book quickly.

    B   She liked the writer.

    C   She enjoyed the story.

19 You will hear two classmates talking about a college trip. Where did they go?

    A   to an art exhibition

    B   to the theatre

    C   to a museum

20 You will hear a woman talking to her son. What does she want her son to do?

    A   collect his sister

    B   prepare his meal

    C   remember his key

Part 5

Questions 21 – 25

For each question, choose the correct answer. You will hear Diane talking to a friend about her birthday presents. What present did each person give her?

Example:

0   mum | C |

People		Presents	
21	uncle	A	bag
22	grandma	B	baseball cap
		C	book
23	sister	D	camera
24	brother	E	chocolates
		F	concert tickets
25	cousin	G	jeans
		H	scarf

TEST 6 SPEAKING

Part 1 (3–4 minutes)

Phase 1

The examiner will ask you and your partner some questions about yourself.
- What's your name?
- How old are you?
- Do you work or are you a student?
- Where do you come from?
- Where do you live?

Phase 2

Now, let's talk about **food**.

A, what's your favourite food?
How often do you cook?

B, what's your favourite meal?
When did you last eat with friends?

Extended response

Now **A**, please tell me something about a popular dish in your country.

> **Extra questions**
> What kind of food is popular in your country?
> When do people usually eat this dish?
> Do you ever cook this food?

Now, let's talk about **friends**.

B, how often do you see your friends?
What do you usually do with your friends?

A, where is a good place to meet new friends?
Do you like to spend time with one friend or a big group of friends?

Extended response

Now, **B**, please tell me something about your best friend.

> **Extra questions**
> How long have you known him/her?
> How did you meet him/her?
> Why do you like him/her?

Part 2 (5–6 minutes)

Phase 1

The examiner will show you some pictures and ask you and your partner to talk about the things they show.

Now, in this part of the test you are going to talk together.
(Turn to the pictures on page 169.)

Here are some pictures that show different kinds of **holidays**.

Do you like these different kinds of holidays? Say why or why not. I'll say that again.
Do you like these different kinds of holidays? Say why or why not.
All right? Now, talk together.

⏱ about 1–2 minutes

The examiner will ask you at least one question each.

Do you think …

… cycling holidays are fun?
… holidays on a boat are interesting?
… cities are exciting?
… beach holidays are boring?
… camping holidays are a good idea?

> **Extra questions**
> Why?/Why not?
> What do you think?

So, **A**, which of these kinds of holidays do you like best?
And you, **B**, which of these kinds of holidays do you like best?

⏱ about 1–2 minutes

Thank you.

Phase 2

Now, do you prefer to go on holiday in the winter or the summer, **B**? (Why)
And what about you, **A**? (Do you prefer to go on holiday in the winter or the summer?) (Why?)

Where would you like to go for your next holiday, **A**? (Why?)
And you, **B**? (Where would you like to go for your next holiday?) (Why?)

⏱ maximum 2 minutes

Thank you. That is the end of the test.

GRAMMAR BANK

There is/are

We use *there is/there are* when we want to say that something exists.

There's a pair of jeans.
There aren't any books.
Is there a mobile phone in your bag?
Are there any plates on the table?

We often use short forms where possible (*there's*, *there isn't*, *there aren't*).

We use *there is/isn't* + *a/an* + noun to talk about one thing (= singular).

There's a bed.
There isn't a pair of trainers on the floor.

Positive

singular	plural
There's (There is) a/an ...	There are two/three/four ... There are some ...

Negative

singular	plural
There isn't (There is not) a/an ...	There aren't two/three/four ... There aren't any ...

Questions

singular	plural
Is there a/an ... ?	Are there any ... ?

Short answers

singular	plural
Yes, there is./No, there isn't.	Yes, there are./No, there aren't.

Practice

1 Complete the short answers.

a A: Is there a chair in your room?
B: Yes, ...

b A: Are there four towels in the bathroom?
B: Yes, ...

c A: Is there a bowl on the table?
B: No, ...

d A: Are there two pillows on the bed?
B: Yes, ...

e A: Are there eight knives in the drawer?
B: No, ...

f A: Is there a key in my bag?
B: No, ...

2 Complete the sentences with *There is* or *There are*.

a .... a pencil case on my desk.
b .... some shelves in the dining room.
c .... two fridges in my brother's kitchen.
d .... a cat on my bed.
e .... a pair of socks on the floor.
f .... three big trees in the garden.

3 Complete the description of Judy's sitting room.

My favourite room in the house is the sitting room. There **(a)**.............. a comfortable sofa and there **(b)**.............. two armchairs. There **(c)**.............. a small coffee table. There **(d)**.............. lots of magazines on the coffee table. There **(e)**.............. a large television in the corner. There **(f)**.............. three pictures on the wall. There **(g)**.............. a black and white photo of my grandparents on a shelf. There **(h)**.............. also lots of books on the shelf.

Countable and uncountable nouns; *some* and *any*

Most common nouns are countable. They have both singular and plural forms.

chair – chairs

Other common nouns are uncountable. They have a singular form, but no plural form.

water   money

Positive: *some*

countable	uncountable
There are **some clothes** on the floor.	There's **some money** in my purse.

Negative: *any*

countable	uncountable
There aren't **any** sandwiches.	There isn't **any** water.

Questions: *any*

countable	uncountable
Are there **any** magazines?	Is there **any** music?

A/An means one and we use it with singular nouns. We use *some* with plural nouns (more than one thing) or for things we can't count.

We use *some*:
- with plural countable nouns.
  *We've got **some books**.*
- with uncountable nouns.
  *Give the cat **some milk**.*

Any often replaces *some* in questions and after negative verbs.
*I want **some** eggs.*
*Do you want **any** eggs?*
*No, I don't want **any** eggs, thanks.*

We use *there is a/an* + noun to talk about one thing.
We use *there are some* + noun to talk about more than one thing.
We use *there is some* + noun to talk about uncountable things.
***There's a man** at the door.*
***There are some posters** on my wall.*
***There is some food** on the table.*

For negatives, we use *there isn't any* + uncountable noun, or *there aren't any* + plural noun.
***There isn't any** water.*
***There aren't any** windows.*

For questions, we change the order of the words.
***There are** some posters on the wall.* → ***Are there** any posters on the wall?*

Practice

1 Are these nouns countable (C) or uncountable (U)?

a	rice	....	e	month	....
b	shoe	....	f	sister	....
c	time	....	g	milk	....
d	furniture	....	h	phone	....

2 Choose the correct words to complete the sentences.
- a There's **some** / **any** fruit on the table.
- b Sam has got **some** / **any** new boots.
- c I don't have **some** / **any** photos on my phone.
- d There isn't **some** / **any** cheese in the fridge.
- e I've got **some** / **any** money in my pocket.
- f There aren't **some** / **any** clean T-shirts in my drawer!

3 Complete the conversation with *some* or *any*.

Sarah: Do you have (a) .... juice, Matt? I'm really thirsty!
Matt: No, sorry, but there's (b) .... milk.
Sarah: Oh. Is there (c) .... cold water in the fridge?
Matt: No, sorry. But there is (d) .... ice.
Sarah: OK. Have you got (e) .... ice cream?
Matt: No, Sarah. There isn't (f) .... food in the house!

Present simple

We use the present simple for habits, for repeated actions and routines, and for things that are always true.

Positive

I/We/You/They	speak.
He/She/It	speak**s**.

Negative

I/We/You/They	**don't** speak.
He/She/It	**doesn't** speak.

questions

Do	I/we/you/they	speak?
Does	he/she/it	speak?

Short answers

Yes,	I/we/you/they	**do**.
	he/she/it	**does**.
No,	I/we/you/they	**don't**.
	he/she/it	**doesn't**.

The third person singular (*He/She/It*) of the present simple positive ends in *-s*.

Some verbs take *-es* or *-ies*.

run – run**s**   write – write**s**   go – go**es**
catch – catch**es**   try – tr**ies**   study – stud**ies**

We use the present simple to talk about:

- facts and things that are always or usually true.
  *Simon **lives** in London.*
  *Cats **like** fish.*

- a habit or routine.
  *He **plays** rugby every Saturday.*

Adverbs of frequency

The present simple can be used with adverbs of frequency: *always, ever, usually, often, sometimes, never*.

Adverbs of frequency say how often something happens.
*I **usually play** video games on Saturday.*
*In summer, I **sometimes go** fishing.*

always   100%
usually
often
sometimes
not often
not usually
never   0%

In a sentence, adverbs of frequency come:

- before the main verb.
  *He **usually takes** photos at home.*

- after the verb *be*.
  *She **is always** nervous before she performs.*

Adverbs of frequency usually appear in the middle of a sentence but can be at the start or the end.
*The trains are **never** late.*
*We **usually** fly our kites on the beach.*
***Sometimes** he plays the piano.*
*Why don't you cook dinner more **often**?*

Practice

1 Complete the conversation with the present simple form of the verbs in brackets.

Ben: What **(a)** .... you .... (do) in your free time?

Fiona: I **(b)** .... (like) dancing and playing the guitar.

Ben: **(c)** .... your brother .... (dance)?

Fiona: No, he doesn't. He **(d)** .... (not like) dancing.

Ben: What **(e)** .... your brother .... (do) in his free time?

Fiona: He likes cycling and running. He **(f)** .... (run) nearly every day.

2 Complete the text with the present simple form of these verbs.

go (×2)   like   not buy   not have
not walk   order   spend   watch

Mandy usually **(a)** .... her weekends with her family. On Friday evenings they sometimes **(b)** .... pizzas from the Italian restaurant near their house. On Saturday mornings she always **(c)** .... to the shops with her sister, but Mandy **(d)** .... usually .... anything expensive. On Saturday evenings Mandy and her family often **(e)** .... a DVD together at home. Most Sundays they **(f)** .... for a walk in the country, but they **(g)** .... very far. On Sunday afternoons, when Mandy **(h)** .... any homework to do, she **(i)** .... listening to music in her room.

3 Choose the correct words to complete the sentences.

a Peter doesn't like the water. He **doesn't often go** / **usually goes** swimming.

b Alex **never** / **always** eats chocolate because he doesn't like sweet things.

c Anna **often plays** / **doesn't often play** basketball. It's her favourite sport.

d Cathy and Terry **always** / **sometimes** listen to the radio, but not every day.

GRAMMAR BANK

e My family **usually / don't often** go to the mountains in the holidays because we love climbing.

f I **always / sometimes** get up early on weekdays. My bus to college is at 7.30 a.m.

4 Rewrite the sentences. Put the adverbs in brackets in the correct place.

a Alice goes sailing on Saturdays. (always)
....
b I play video games in the morning. (never)
....
c Pizzas aren't expensive. (usually)
....
d My sister plays tennis. (often)
....
e Football club is on Saturday morning. (always)
....
f Ryan doesn't watch television. (often)
....

Much/Many

Much is a quantity word meaning *a large amount of*. We use *much* with uncountable nouns in questions and negatives.
*How **much** free time does she have?*
*They didn't have **much** fun at the party.*

Many is a quantity word meaning *a large number (of)*. We use *many* with plural countable nouns in questions and negatives.
*How **many** students go to chess club?*
*She doesn't have **many** books.*

Practice

1 Complete the questions with *much* or *many*.

a How .... pairs of shoes have you got?
b How .... money do you spend on snacks?
c How .... photos have you got on your phone?
d How .... time do you spend sleeping?
e How .... times a month do you eat pasta?
f How .... water do you drink every day?

2 Complete the email. Write one word for each gap.

New Message

Hi Chloe,

Do you **(a)**.................. to come to a photography class with me? I **(b)**.................. every Wednesday evening. There aren't **(c)**.................. students in the class and they're all very nice. It doesn't cost **(d)**.................. money – it's only £5 a month. It starts at 5.30 p.m. and **(e)**.................. at 6.30 p.m. What **(f)**.................. you think?

Zoe

Present continuous

Positive

I	'm	sing**ing**.
He/She/It	's	
We/You/They	're	

Negative

I	'm not	sing**ing**.
He/She/It	isn't	
We/You/They	aren't	

Questions

Am	I	sing**ing**?
Is	he/she/it	
Are	we/you/they	

GRAMMAR BANK

Short answers

Yes,	I	**am**.
	he/she/it	**is**.
	we/you/they	**are**.
No,	I	**'m not**.
	he/she/it	**isn't**.
	we/you/they	**aren't**.

We use the present continuous to talk about:

- something happening now.
  Wait a minute. I'm texting Joe.
  Sophie's not doing anything at the moment.
  What are you doing right now?
- temporary situations.
  Mr Evans is teaching us maths because Miss Hill is on holiday.
  Tom isn't playing in the team today because he's ill.
- something happening in a picture/photo.
  In this photo, I'm sitting next to my best friend.

We use the verb *be* (*am*, *is*, *are*) or its short forms (*I'm*, *you're*, *he's*, *she's*, etc.) + main verb + *-ing*.

We often use the present continuous with these time phrases: *right now*, *at the moment*, *now*, *today*.

Remember there are spelling rules for making the *-ing* form.

most verbs	add *-ing*	catch – catching
verbs ending in *-e*	remove the final *-e*	take – taking
verbs ending in *-ie*	change *-ie* to *-y*	lie – lying
verbs ending in one vowel and one consonant	double the final consonant	hit – hitting

Practice

1 Complete the short answers.

a **A:** Are you writing an email?
B: No, I .... I'm texting Ollie.

b **A:** Is Tom watching the match?
B: Yes, he .... But his team's losing!

c **A:** Are you listening to music?
B: Yes, I .... It's my favourite song.

d **A:** Are we winning?
B: No, we .... We're playing badly today.

e **A:** Are they cooking?
B: Yes, they .... They're making dinner!

2 Complete the sentences with the present continuous form of the verbs in brackets.

a At the moment we .... (learn) how to make chocolate cake.

b The boys .... (not do) their homework.

c Amira .... (look) for her phone. Can you help?

d We .... (play) a video game. Do you want to play too?

e I .... (not surf) the internet. This is work!

f My little brother .... (use) my laptop right now.

Present simple and Present continuous

We use the present simple for a regular or repeated activity.
My mum usually leaves the house at 8.30 a.m.

And we use the present continuous for things happening now or around now and temporary situations.
She's leaving the house now.

Practice

1 Choose the correct words to complete the sentences.

a Can you phone again in half an hour? **I'm chatting** / **chat** to my sister online.

b **I'm writing** / **write** about ten emails every day.

c Every time you **'re going** / **go** to this cinema, you get a free coffee.

d I haven't got time to talk now. **I'm trying** / **try** to finish my art project.

e Look! **I'm standing** / **stand** on one leg!

f **I'm usually taking** / **I usually take** lots of photos when I'm on holiday.

2 Complete the email with the present simple or present continuous form of these verbs.

be	enjoy	have (×2)	rain	stand
stay	visit			

New Message

Hi Lizzy!
(a) .... you .... a good time in France?
I **(b)** .... my holiday in Greece. The weather **(c)** .... great here – I'm sure it **(d)** .... back home in Ireland right now!
The campsite we **(e)** .... in is really cool. The people are friendly and they **(f)** .... a good café with really nice music. Today we **(g)** .... the Parthenon in Athens. I **(h)** .... in front of it right now. It looks awesome!
Speak soon,
Amy

Question words with the present continuous

Question words go before the verb *be*.

question word	be	subject	verb
What	am	I	do**ing**?
Where	are	they	stay**ing**?
Who	is	she	talk**ing** to?
How	are	you	go**ing** to France?

Practice

1 Complete the questions with the present simple or present continuous form of the verbs in brackets.

a How much fruit .... you .... (eat) every day?
b Why .... the baby .... (cry) now? Is she hungry?
c Which café .... you .... (visit) the most?
d What video game .... Leah .... (play) at the moment?
e When .... you usually .... (watch) television?
f Where .... you .... (go) at the moment?

Past simple

We use the past simple to talk about things that happened in the past. We use it for completed actions that are not happening now.
*Jack **helped** Anna with her homework.*

To be

We use *was* and *were* (the past tense of *be*) to talk about the past.

Positive

I/He/She/It	**was**	excited.
We/You/They	**were**	on holiday.

We usually use short forms in negative sentences.

Negative

I/He/She/It	**wasn't**	excited.
We/You/They	**weren't**	on holiday.

Regular verbs

The past simple of regular verbs ends in -*ed*. Sometimes the spelling changes.
talk – talked   *arrive – arrived*
study – studied   *travel – travelled*

Positive

I/He/She/It/We/You/They	walk**ed**.

We make negative sentences with *didn't* and the base form of the verb.
We don't add -*ed* to the verb in negative sentences.

Negative

I/He/She/It/We/You/They	**didn't walk**.

Irregular verbs

Some verbs have a different form in the past simple.
be – was   *buy – bought*   *come – came*
eat – ate   *find – found*   *go – went*
have – had   *know – knew*   *meet – met*
read – read   *see – saw*   *win – won*

GRAMMAR BANK

Positive

| I/He/She/It/We/You/They | went | to the beach. |

Negative

| I/He/She/It/We/You/They | didn't go | to the beach. |

Time expressions with the past simple

We often use these time expressions when we talk about the past: *yesterday*, *last week*, *last year*, *two weeks ago*, *a month ago*, *in 2018*, etc.

I saw him **yesterday**.
We went to the mountains **last weekend**.
I started my Saturday job **a year ago**.

Practice

1 Choose the correct words to complete the blog.

> **mycollegespace.com**
>
> My first day at college **(a) was / were** great. The classes **(b) were / weren't** difficult, so I'm not worried. But they **(c) was / were** very interesting, so I **(d) was / wasn't** bored at all. The other students **(e) were / weren't** nice and I've already got some new friends. What about you? **(f) Was / Were** your first day good?

2 Complete the sentences with these verbs

> arrived   bought   met   took   went   wore

- **a** Michael .... his girlfriend when he was on holiday.
- **b** Luke .... a new tennis racket last Saturday.
- **c** We all .... at the cinema at the same time.
- **d** I .... an amazing photo of my dog yesterday.
- **e** Jenny .... her orange trainers today.
- **f** My cousin .... to Brazil last month.

3 Complete the sentences with the past simple form of the verbs in brackets.

- **a** Last summer John's dad .... (travel) to South America for work.
- **b** The concert .... (start) at 7.30 p.m. and .... (finish) at 10.30 p.m.
- **c** Laura .... (not study) for her exam and so she .... (not pass) it.
- **d** The children .... (run) all the way home because they .... (be) late.
- **e** My grandma .... (give) me some beautiful earrings for my birthday.
- **f** Everyone .... (stop) work when the boss .... (come) into the office.

Past simple questions and short answers

The verb goes at the start of the question.

To be

Yes/No questions

| Was | I/he/she/it | happy? |
| Were | we/you/they | in the café? |

Short answers

Yes,	I/he/she/it	was
	we/you/they	were.
No,	I/he/she/it	wasn't.
	we/you/they	weren't.

Question words go before the verb.
Where was the hotel?
Who were your favourite players this season?
What was your grandfather's name?

Regular and irregular verbs

We don't add *-ed* to the verb in questions. We change the word order and insert *Did* before the main verb.

Yes/No questions

| Did | I/he/she/it/we/you/they | arrive?
go? |

Short answers

Yes,	I/he/she/it/we/you/they	**did**.
No,		**didn't**.

Wh- questions

Who **did**	I/he/she/it/we/you/they	**know**?
Where **did**		**live**?

Practice

1 Put the words in the correct order to make questions.

a finish / you / book / Did / the
   ....?

b yesterday evening / did / Who / you / meet
   ....?

c like / the / you / film / Did
   ....?

d this afternoon / Did / leave early / you
   ....?

e interesting / Was / music lesson / your
   ....

2 Complete the questions. Write one word for each gap. Then match the questions (1–6) with the answers (A–F).

1 .... did you go?
2 .... it snow?
3 .... it very cold?
4 .... you happy there?
5 .... did you get home?
6 .... you have a great time?

A Last Friday.
B Yes, I did.
C No, it didn't!
D Yes, it was.
E Switzerland.
F Yes, I was.

3 Complete the email. Write one word for each gap.

New Message

Hi Charlie,

How **(a)**............ your holiday in Scotland? **(b)**............ you do anything exciting? Last August we **(c)**............ a short holiday in Edinburgh. Did you **(d)**............ there? There **(e)**............ a lot of people in Edinburgh in August because there was a big festival. When we arrived, our hotel **(f)**............ full! We **(g)**............ find any rooms to stay in but in the end my dad **(h)**............ a campsite and they **(i)**............ a caravan for us. It **(j)**............ fun – a camping holiday and an Arts festival at the same time!

(k)............ you visit Edinburgh Castle when you were there? Or the National Gallery? I **(l)**............ both of those.

Write soon,

Love from

Penny

Comparative and superlative adjectives

type	comparative	superlative
short adjectives *cheap, old, young* *Markets are **cheap**.*	add *-er* *cheaper, older, younger* *Markets are cheap**er** than shops.*	add *-est* *the cheap**est**, the old**est**, the young**est*** *Markets are the cheap**est** place to shop.*
adjectives ending in *-e* *nice, wide* *This cake is really **nice**.*	add *-r* *nicer, wider* *This cake is **nicer than** that one.*	add *-st* *the nice**st**, the wide**st*** *This cake is **the nicest** I've ever had.*
one-syllable adjectives ending in one vowel and one consonant *fat, big* *That is a **big** mistake.*	double the final consonant, add *-er* *fatter, bigger* *That is a **bigger** mistake than the one Jack made.*	double the final consonant, add *-est* *the fat**test**, the big**gest*** *That is the **biggest** mistake you've made.*
two-syllable adjectives ending in *-y* *easy, happy* *This homework is **easy**.*	delete *-y*, add *-ier* *eas**ier**, happ**ier*** *This homework is **easier than** yesterday's homework.*	delete *-y*, add *-iest* *the eas**iest**, the happ**iest*** *This homework is **the easiest** homework ever!*
long adjectives *interesting* *That book was **interesting**.*	*more/less* + adjective *more interesting* *That book is **more interesting than** the other one.*	*the most/the least* + adjective *the most interesting* *That is the most interesting book I've read this year.*
irregular adjectives *good, bad, far* *Today was a good day.*	*better, worse, farther/further* *Today was **better than** yesterday.*	*the best, the worst, the farthest/the furthest* *Today was **the best** day ever!*

Note: The comparative of *fun* is *more fun*.
*Shopping with friends is **more fun** than shopping alone.*

Comparative adjectives

We use comparative adjectives + *than* to compare two people or things.
*The black jeans are **cheaper than** the white ones.*
*Your smartphone is **nicer than** mine.*
*The new shop assistant is **funnier than** the last one.*
*Markets are **more interesting than** shops.*
*The food is **better** here **than** in the other café.*

Sometimes the second person/thing is implied and *than* isn't necessary.
*The shops are always **busier** in the summer.*

We can also use comparative adjectives with *have got* for physical features.
*I've got **darker** hair than you.*
*You've got **bigger** feet than me.*
*Harry's got **curlier** hair than Mark.*

Practice

1 **Write the comparative form of the adjectives.**

a wide ....
b pretty ....
c comfortable ....
d hot ....
e tall ....
f boring ....
g thin ....
h light ....

GRAMMAR BANK

2 Complete the sentences with the comparative form of the adjectives in brackets.

a The shops are always _____ (busy) on Saturdays.
b This week it's _____ (sunny) than last week.
c My brother is _____ (young) than me, but I'm _____ (short) than him.
d This park is _____ (beautiful) in the spring.
e A sandwich is _____ (cheap) than a pizza.
f Maths this year is _____ (difficult) than last year.

3 Complete the article with the comparative form of the adjectives in brackets. Use *than* where necessary.

City or small town?

For me, living in the city is **(a)** _____ (interesting) living in a small town. Cities are **(b)** _____ (big), and the shops in the city centre are **(c)** _____ (good) the shops in small towns. Most cities are **(d)** _____ (crowded) small towns and the streets are usually **(e)** _____ (busy). But there are also lots of buses and trains, so it's **(f)** _____ (easy) to get about.

Superlative adjectives

We use superlative adjectives to compare one thing or person to others in a group. We use *the* before the superlative adjective.

*I'm **the youngest** shop assistant.*
*He's **the nicest** customer.*
*We always choose **the biggest** pizza.*
*Matt tells **the funniest** jokes.*
*She bought **the most expensive** skateboard.*
*This is **the best** restaurant.*

We often use these expressions after superlative adjectives: *in the world*, *in the class*, *in the school*, *in the town*.
*The best music shop **in the town**.*
*The wettest country **in the world**.*

We can also use superlative adjectives with *have got* for physical features.
*I've got **the darkest** hair.*
*You've got **the biggest** feet.*
*Harry's got **the curliest** hair.*

Practice

1 Write the superlative form of the adjectives.

a quiet _____
b fat _____
c large _____
d big _____
e good _____
f important _____
g sunny _____
h famous _____

2 Complete the sentences with these superlative adjectives.

---

the happiest   the heaviest
the most expensive   the shortest
the slowest   the wettest

---

a Last week was _____ week I can remember. It rained every day.
b We were _____ runners in the race. We finished last!
c My little sister is _____ person in my family. We're all taller than her.
d This is _____ bicycle in the shop. It costs £400!
e I won the marathon on Saturday! It was _____ day of my life.
f My history book is _____ book in my bag. It's 2 kilos!

GRAMMAR BANK

3 Complete the blog. Write one word for each gap.

A trip to the zoo

Yesterday I visited the zoo and I think it was **(a)** .... best day of my week. I saw some great animals and learnt a lot! For example, the biggest animal **(b)** .... the world is the blue whale. There isn't a whale in that zoo, but there are some other big animals, like elephants and bears.

For me, the **(c)** .... interesting animals there are the snakes. There are lots of different snakes, all in a special snake house to keep them, and us, safe. Some snakes, like the cobra, are **(d)** .... dangerous than others. The monkeys are very popular animals, more popular **(e)** .... the snakes! One quite strange animal in the zoo is a rabbit! It isn't big or dangerous, but it's **(f)** .... longer ears than most rabbits – about 60 centimetres long!

Past continuous

We form the past continuous with *was* or *were* + the *-ing* form of the verb.

Positive

I/He/She/It	was	eat**ing**.
We/You/They	were	

Negative

I/He/She/It	wasn't	eat**ing**.
We/You/They	weren't	

questions

Was	I/he/she/it	eat**ing**?
Were	we/you/they	

short answers

Yes,	I/he/she/it	**was**.
	we/you/they	**were**.
No,	I/he/she/it	**wasn't**.
	we/you/they	**weren't**.

We use the past continuous:
- for actions happening at a particular time in the past.
  *He **was doing** his homework this morning.*
  *She **wasn't reading** her book last night.*
  *What **were** you **doing** at ten o'clock this morning?*
- to set the scene in a story.
  *It was a dark night and it **was raining** heavily.*
- for two or more actions happening at the same time in the past.
  *They **were playing** video games and **watching** a film at the same time!*

We often use the past continuous with time phrases like *yesterday*, *last weekend*, *at three o'clock* and *at midday*.
*Mum was working **last weekend**.*
*We were eating **at three o'clock yesterday**.*

Practice

1 Complete the sentences with *was*, *were*, *wasn't* or *weren't*.

a Alan .... playing his guitar.
b What .... you doing at 9 a.m. this morning?
c I .... playing football yesterday – I wasn't in the team.
d Why .... Rebecca crying?
e We .... cycling – we were running.
f Steve and Sue .... visiting a museum.

2 Complete the conversation with the past continuous form of the verbs in brackets.

Kim: Hi, Joe. I didn't see you at the park on Saturday. What **(a)**............... you .... ? (do)

Joe: I **(b)**............... (play) chess with the chess club. There's a competition soon, so we **(c)**............... (practise) our game.

Kim: Oh, good luck then! Well, we had a game of football in the park. My team **(d)**............... (win), when suddenly Fran fell and hit her head.

Joe: Oh dear! Did she cry?

Kim: No, in the beginning, she **(e)**............... (not move) at all. We were very worried. Ann and Cathy **(f)**............... (put) water on her face. Then she woke up. She was OK!

Joe: That's good! It's lucky you **(g)**............... (not play) an important match!

Past continuous and Past simple

We use the past simple and past continuous in the same sentence to talk about an action that was in progress (past continuous) when another action happened (past simple). We use *when* before the action in the past simple.
*We **were eating** breakfast **when** they **came** in.*
***When** they **came** in, we **were eating** breakfast.*

Practice

1 Choose the correct words to complete the sentences.

a I **read / was reading** when they **came back / were coming back** from the party.

b Pauline **didn't listen / wasn't listening** when I **asked / was asking** her to help me.

c They **chatted / were chatting** online when Peter **arrived / was arriving**.

d We **had / were having** coffee when we **heard / were hearing** a terrible noise.

e Jim **checked / was checking** his emails when Mia **called / was calling**.

f They **waited / were waiting** for the bus when they **saw / were seeing** a famous film star.

2 Complete the questions with the past continuous or past simple form of these verbs.

| arrive | hurt | meet | rain | run | watch |

a Were they having dinner when you .... home?

b Why .... you .... when I saw you yesterday?

c .... it .... when you left last night?

d .... you .... a film when I rang?

e Was Kelly living in London when you first .... her?

f I was skiing in the Alps when I .... my leg.

3 Complete the blog. Write one word for each gap.

The transport museum

Last weekend it **(a)**............... raining and my brother and I **(b)**............... feeling a bit bored. We **(c)**............... looking for something interesting to do, and Dad suggested going to the Transport Museum in town. We were **(d)**............... very excited, because we **(e)**............... hoping to do something more interesting! But we **(f)**............... not have anything better to do, so we went there on Saturday afternoon. And it **(g)**............... amazing! Not boring at all! There **(h)**............... all kinds of transport – cars, buses, trams and trains, bicycles, motorbikes – everything! When we arrived at the museum, a man **(i)**............... explaining what everything was and why it was important. We **(j)**............... a great afternoon!

Defining relative clauses

We use defining relative clauses to give important information about the person or thing we are talking about.
*That's the boy **who** won the race.*
*We visited a museum **that** was amazing.*

We use *who/that* to refer to people.
*That's the boy **who** found my keys.*
*Is Katy the girl **that** your brother likes?*

We use *which/that* to refer to things or animals.
*They found some treasure **which** was really old.*
*The new dog **that** we've got is black and white.*

We can use defining relative clauses to make two sentences into one.
The film was about a boy. He lived in China.
*The film was about a boy **who** lived in China.*

A defining relative clause is essential to the sense of the sentence, it can't be removed.
*I met the man **who** wrote this book.*
I met the man. (Which man?)

Practice

1 Choose the correct words to complete the sentences.

a Emma's the girl **who / which** got the best marks in the test.
b Are they the boys **that / which** live next door to you?
c Frogs are animals **who / which** can live on land and in water.
d Is there a dress **that / who** you like in this shop?
e My brothers are the ones **who / which** have got fair hair – my hair's dark.
f Are those all the books **that / who** you need?

Be going to

We use *be going to* to talk about intentions for the future or things we have decided to do.
*I**'m going to stay** with my cousins next year.*
*They**'re going to take** lots of photos on holiday.*
***Are** you **going to talk** to him?*

We use the verb *be* + *going to* + the infinitive of the main verb.

Positive

I	'm	going to stay.
He/She/It	is	
We/You/They	are	

Negative

I	'm not	going to stay.
He/She/It	isn't	
We/You/They	aren't	

questions

Am	I	going to stay?
Is	he/she/it	
Were	we/you/they	

short answers

Yes,	I	am.
	he/she/it	is.
	we/you/they	are.
No,	I	'm not.
	I/he/she/it	isn't.
	we/you/they	aren't.

We often use *be going to* for future plans and intentions which we aren't completely sure about.
*Sandra's **going to meet** some of her friends soon.*
*Are you **going to take** the bus to the airport or the train?*

Practice

1 Put the words in the correct order to make sentences.

a to / across the lake / going / We're / sail
   ....
b is / Barbara / to / a horse / ride / going
   ....
c find / aren't / You / to / your phone / going
   ....
d to the café / to / They / going / walk / are
   ....
e meet / not / I'm / going / Tom / to
   ....
f Louis / leave / is / to / going / at 5 o'clock
   ....

2 Complete the questions with the correct form of *be going to* and the verbs in brackets. Then complete the short answers.

a **A:** Is your dad .... (buy) a new car this year?
   B: Yes, ...
b **A:** Are Pete and Andy .... (learn) Spanish?
   B: No, ...
c **A:** Are we .... (see) Nina tonight?
   B: Yes, ...
d **A:** Is your brother .... (come) home this weekend?
   B: No, ...
e **A:** Are you .... (travel) to Holland by plane?
   B: Yes, ...
f **A:** Are you .... (join) the photography club?
   B: No, ...

Will

Positive

| I/He/She/It/We/You/They | will | win. |

Negative

| I/He/She/It/We/You/They | won't | win. |

questions

| Will | I/he/she/it/we/you/they | win? |

short answers

| Yes, | I/he/she/it/we/you/they | will. |
| No, | I/he/she/it/we/you/they | won't. |

We use *will* or *won't* (*will not*) to talk about predictions or things we think or hope will happen.
*She**'ll enjoy** the boat trip.*
*It **won't be** very busy at the bus station.*

We often use *I think/I don't think* before *will*.
***I think** she**'ll come** later.*
***I don't think** you**'ll like** it.*

We also use *will/won't* to talk about facts or certainty in the future.
*It **will be** very hot in Seville in August.*
*The dogs **will bark** when the postman comes.*

Note: Don't forget short forms when we use *I/you/he/she/we/they*.

*I will – **I'll**   she will – **she'll**   we will – **we'll***

Practice

1 Complete the sentences with *will/'ll* or *won't* and the verbs in brackets.

a We .... (take) the bus because it's cheaper.
b Next summer my sister .... (be) eighteen.
c I think you .... (learn) a lot in the computer class.
d I .... (not do) my homework today because I feel tired.
e .... they .... (find) the information easily?
f I don't think Sam .... (come) today because it's raining.

GRAMMAR BANK

2 Complete the conversations. Use the correct form of *be going to* or *will* and the verbs in brackets.

a **A:** The supermarket is closed. What .... we .... (do)?
   B: There's another one near the sports centre. I think it .... (be) open.

b **A:** I .... (meet) Sally at the cinema later. Do you want to come?
   B: Sorry, I can't. I .... (help) my mum with the cooking.

c **A:** Freya .... (stay) with her aunt in the Monte Carlo this summer.
   B: Cool. I'm sure she .... (have) a great time.

Present continuous for future

We use the present continuous to talk about definite plans or arrangements for the near future.
We're flying to France this evening.
I'm taking the bus to the beach later.
Are you coming to the park this afternoon?

We often use these future time phrases with the present continuous: *this afternoon, later, tonight, this evening, tomorrow, next week, at the weekend, in the summer, next year.*

Note: We don't usually say *going to go*. We use the present continuous.
We're going to go to the cinema tonight.
We're going to the cinema tonight.
She's going to Argentina next year.

Practice

1 Complete the sentences with the present continuous form of these verbs.

| come   get   have   leave   play   take |

a We .... my grandma to the beach next weekend.
b I .... for the airport at 7.30 a.m. tomorrow.
c They .... married next month.
d All my friends .... to my party next week.
e I .... tennis this afternoon.
f Pat .... a barbecue on Sunday.

2 Choose the correct words to complete the email.

Hi!
I'm having a great time in Brighton with my classmates. We **(a) 'll leave / 're leaving** for the train station soon because we **(b) 're going / 'll go** to London for the day. The train journey **(c) will / won't** be very long – only about an hour. In London, most of us **(d) are / is** going to visit the Science Museum. Our science teacher **(e) is / isn't** coming with us and he **(f) 's going to / 'll** be our guide. He says it's a brilliant museum, so I think it **(g) will / won't** be really interesting! The students in the tennis club **(h) don't come / aren't coming** with us because they've got a match.
I'll send you photos from the museum!
Bye for now,
Sandy

Can/Could

Positive

I/He/She/It/We/You/They	can	sing.
	could	

Negative

I/He/She/It/We/You/They	can't	sing.
	couldn't	

Questions

Can	I/he/she/it/we/you/they	sing?
Could		

Short answers

Yes,	I/he/she/it/we/you/they	can.
		could.
No,	I/he/she/it/we/you/they	can't.
		couldn't.

We use *can* + infinitive to talk about ability and possibility in the present.

Can – ability

In this case *can* means 'be (physically) able to' do something.

*I **can play** table tennis, but I'm not very good.*
*The students in my class **can't speak** English very well.*
***Can** you **play** the piano? Yes, I **can**./No, I **can't**.*

Can – possibility

In this case *can* means 'it is possible'.

*Learning to surf **can be** difficult.*
*Football **can** be fun for girls, too.*
*That girl **can't be** in our class, she's really young.*

We use *could* + infinitive to talk about ability in the past.

*Matt **could swim** when he was six years old.*
*Some people **couldn't hit** the ball very hard.*
*He **could practise** the guitar all afternoon.*

Practice

1 Write short answers.

a Can he ride a horse? ✓
B: ....

b Could he play tennis at school? ✗
B: ....

c Can you learn badminton at the sports centre? ✗
B: ....

d Could you play table tennis three years ago? ✓
B: ....

e Can trainers cost over £50? ✓
B: ....

f Can dogs go in this park? ✗
B: ....

2 Complete the conversations with *can*, *can't*, *could* or *couldn't*.

a A: .... we use our skateboards in this park?
B: No, we .... Skateboarding .... be dangerous for other people.

b A: .... you speak French?
B: Yes, I .... , but I only started last year. I .... speak French at all before that.

c A: .... you swim when you were five years old?
B: Yes, I .... , but my brother .... swim until he was ten.

Have to/Had to

Positive

I/We/You/They	have to	train every day.
	had to	
He/She/It	has to	
	had to	

Negative

I/We/You/They	don't have to	train every day.
	didn't have to	
He/She/It	doesn't have to	
	didn't have to	

questions

Do	I/we/you/they	have to	train every day?
Did			
Does	he/she/it		
Did			

We use *have to* + infinitive to talk about general rules in the present or something that is necessary.

*You **have to wear** a helmet when you're cycling.*
*He **has to wear** special trainers to run fast.*

We use *had to* + infinitive to talk about general rules in the past or something that was necessary.

*My mum **had to wear** a tie when she was at secondary school.*
*The runners **had to drink** a lot of water during the marathon.*

We use *don't/doesn't have to* (present) and *didn't have to* (past) when there is no obligation or something isn't necessary.

*You **don't have to buy** a skateboard. You can use mine.*
*I **didn't have to buy** a skateboard. I used my friend's.*

GRAMMAR BANK

Practice

1 Choose the correct words to complete the sentences.

a I **had to** / **have to** leave early yesterday because I was ill.

b You **have to** / **don't have to** come to all the classes, but they're very useful.

c We **had to** / **didn't have to** buy any books because they were in the library.

d Tim **have to** / **has to** study very hard for his exams.

e In the swimming club we **have to** / **has to** wear black swimsuits.

f Lily **has to** / **doesn't have to** get up early at the weekend because there are no classes.

2 Complete the sentences with the correct form of *have to*.

a .... children .... wear a uniform at this school?

b I .... go shopping yesterday because I needed new shoes.

c Toby .... study in the library every evening because it's very noisy at home.

d You .... wear special clothes. You can wear anything comfortable.

e .... you .... pay for the coffee yesterday or was it free?

f Jody .... buy food because her mother always cooks for her.

Present perfect

Positive

I/We/You/They	have	seen a snake.
He/She/It	has	

Negative

I/We/You/They	haven't	seen a snake.
He/She/It	hasn't	

questions

Have	I/we/you/they	seen a snake?
Has	he/she/it	

short answers

Yes,	I/we/you/they	**have**.
	he/she/it	**has.**
No,	I/we/you/they	**haven't**.
	he/she/it	**hasn't**.

We use the present perfect (*have/has* + past participle) to talk about experiences in our lives up to now. We do not say when the experience was.

He**'s travelled** in the desert. (but we are not saying when)
They **haven't seen** snow.

We use *have/has* + the past participle of the main verb. We usually use the short forms of *have/has*: *'ve, 's, haven't* and *hasn't*.

We**'ve finished** our work.
Tom**'s seen** a lion.
I **haven't been** to New York.
Jane **hasn't arrived**.

For the past participle of regular verbs, we add *-ed*.
climb – climb**ed**   cook – cook**ed**

For some irregular verbs, the past participle is the same as the past simple.
put – put – put   read – read – read

Fo other irregular verbs, the past participle has a different form.
see – saw – seen   swim – swam – swum
write – wrote – written

Note: The verb *go* has two past participles (*gone* and *been*) with different meanings.

She's **gone** to Australia. (She went and is still there.)
She's **been** to Australia. (She went there and then left.)

Practice

1 Complete the sentences with 've or 's and the past participle of the verbs in brackets.

  a They .... (join) the chess club.
  b You .... (miss) the bus.
  c We .... (see) the famous lake.
  d He .... (make) dinner for us.
  e I .... (find) a wallet.
  f She .... (write) three emails today.

2 Make the sentences in Exercise 1 negative.

3 Complete the sentences with *have/has gone* or *have/has been*.

  a Penny isn't here. She .... to Sally's house.
  b This is an interesting museum. .... you .... here before?
  c I .... to Australia. I had a holiday there last year.
  d My parents .... to Rome for the weekend, so I'm looking after the dog.
  e .... Richard .... to the concert? He's not answering his phone.

4 Complete the questions with the present perfect form of the verbs in brackets. Then complete the short answers.

  a **A:** .... (you/read) this book?
     B: No, I ....
  b **A:** .... (he/enjoy) his birthday?
     B: Yes, he ....
  c **A:** .... (they/have) a nice weekend?
     B: Yes, ...
  d **A:** .... (Carol/take) any food with her?
     B: No, ...
  e **A:** .... (John and Amy/see) the elephants?
     B: Yes, ...

Present perfect with *ever* and *never*

Have	I/we/you/they	ever	tried Korean food?
Has	he/she/it		

I/We/You/They	have	never	tried Korean food.
He/She/It	has		

We use the present perfect with *ever* or *never* to talk about experiences in your life up to now.

We use *ever* in questions, to ask if something has happened. There is no specific time phrase in the question.

Have you **ever swum** in the rain?
Has he **ever been** to Turkey?

We use *never* with the positive form of the verb to say something hasn't happened. *Ever* and *never* go between *have/has* and the past participle.

She**'s never skied** in the Alps.
We**'ve never stayed** in a campsite.
Luke**'s never slept** under the stars.

Practice

1 Rewrite the sentences using *ever* or *never*.

  a Have you climbed a mountain?
     ....
  b He has lost his trainers.
     ....
  c We have had a barbecue in our garden.
     ....
  d Has she run in a race?
     ....
  e I have swum in a lake.
     ....
  f Have they tried snake meat?
     ....

2 Complete the article with the present perfect form of these verbs.

| arrive | do | learn | never | not speak |
| travel | teach | | | |

El Camino Language and Culture in Spain

Twenty young students from England **(a)** .... at our language and culture activity camp in the mountains near Madrid. Here's what they're saying.

Katy: Some of us **(b)** .... to Spain before, so it's an exciting a new experience.

Fred: I **(c)** .... lots of new words in Spanish already.

Bobby: We **(d)** .... lots of great activities! My new friend José **(e)** .... me how to ride a horse.

Ewan: I **(f)** .... to my mum all week, but I'm fine!'

Advice: should

Positive

| I/He/She/It/We/You/They | should | eat healthy food. |

Negative

| I/He/She/It/We/You/They | shouldn't | eat junk food. |

questions

| Should | I/he/she/it/we/you/they | eat junk food? |

We use *should* + the infinitive of the main verb to give or ask for advice, or make a recommendation.
*You **should do** more exercise.*
***Should** I **buy** this T-shirt?*

We use the negative *shouldn't* + the infinitive of the main verb to say we don't think it's a good idea to do something.
*You **shouldn't eat** a lot of fried food.*
*You **shouldn't play** computer games every night.*

Practice

1 Complete the advice with *should* or *shouldn't*.

a A: I'm thirsty.
   B: You .... drink some water.

b A: I feel sick.
   B: You .... eat any more chocolate.

c A: My friend Marion loves jewellery.
   B: You .... get her some earrings as a present.

d A: My shoes are very dirty.
   B: You .... clean them.

e A: I feel really tired!
   B: You .... go shopping.

f A: I've haven't got much money.
   B: You .... buy any more clothes.

2 Complete the questions with *should* and these verbs.

| choose | cook | go | leave | text | wear |

a .... I .... you or call you when I arrive?

b What time .... we .... the hotel for the airport?

c How .... I .... the eggs?

d Where .... we .... on holiday this year?

e .... I .... chocolate or strawberry ice cream?

f What .... I .... to the party?

First conditional

if + present tense	*will/won't* + infinitive
If my dad **opens** a café,	I**'ll help** him.
If you **eat** lots of sweets now,	you **won't be** hungry at dinner time.

We use *if* + present simple + *will/may/can/could* + infinitive for:

- describing possible future situations.
  *If we **arrive** late, we **won't get** a table in the restaurant.*
  *If we **hang out** in a café, we **could make** some new friends.*
- making threats.
  *If you **don't hurry**, I'll go without you.*
  *If you **eat** all of that pizza, **you'll feel** sick.*
- making promises.
  *If you **win** the race, I **may buy** you a present.*
  *If you **eat** a healthy meal, you**'ll feel** better.*

We use *if* + present simple + *should* to make suggestions and give advice.
*If you**'re** tired, you **should go** to bed.*
*If you **go** swimming, you **should take** your goggles.*

We use a comma when *if* comes at the beginning of the sentence.
***If** she wins the competition, she'll be very happy.*
(situation)   (consequence)

We don't use a comma when *if* comes in the middle of the sentence.
*She'll be very happy **if** she wins the competition.*
(consequence)   (situation)

Practice

1 Choose the correct words to complete the sentences.

  a If **it's** / **will be** nice weather, we'll go to the park.
  b If you **don't follow** / **won't follow** my directions, you'll get lost.
  c I **buy** / **'ll buy** a pizza if I've got enough money.
  d If Will **doesn't finish** / **won't finish** the exam, he won't pass.
  e She **isn't** / **won't be** tired if she sleeps all afternoon.
  f If you **do** / **'ll do** well in your exam, you'll be really happy.

2 Complete the first conditional sentences. Use the correct form of the verbs in brackets.

  a If we .... (leave) home now, we .... (be) there by 4 p.m.
  b We .... (let) you know if Kieran .... (not arrive).
  c You .... (be) thirsty if you .... (not take) any water.
  d Katy .... (call) me if she .... (need) my help.
  e If I .... (visit) my grandparents, they .... (be) very happy.
  f I .... (buy) you lunch if dad .... (give) me some money.

SPEAKING BANK

You take the Speaking test with a partner, and there are two examiners. One examiner speaks to you, and the other examiner just listens. There are two parts to the test. Each part has two phases. The whole test takes 8–10 minutes.

Part 1 Phase 1

You answer simple questions about your name, age and where you live.

Exam help

- These questions are always the same, and you already know the answers, so practise answering them clearly and confidently.
- Remember, you only need to give short answers to the questions in Phase 1.

Useful language

Giving personal information

My name's …
I'm … years old
I come from …
I live in the city centre.
I live in a city/town/village.

Part 1 Phase 2

In this part of the test, you answer some personal questions about two different things, for example your family, your school, your daily life or what you do in your free time.

Exam help

- You can give short answers to these questions but when the examiner says, 'Tell me something about …' you should give a longer answer.
- If the examiner says 'Tell me about your favourite …', don't just say what it is. Explain your reasons for liking it, and also your reasons for not liking other things.
- Always try to think of something interesting to say.
- Think about the tense you're going to use. The question may be about the present, past or future.
- Speak clearly so that both examiners can hear what you say.
- If you don't understand the question, ask the examiner to repeat it.

Useful language

Likes and dislikes

I enjoy … because …
On Tuesdays I play basketball/go swimming.
On Saturdays I go shopping/meet my friends …
I like/love/enjoy …
I don't like/hate …
I'm good/brilliant at …
I'm OK/not good at …
It's amazing/brilliant/cool!
My favourite … is … because …

Asking the examiner to repeat

Sorry, I don't understand.
Could you say that again, please?
Can you repeat that, please?

Practice Part 1

1 Complete the sentences with information about yourself.
1. My name's ……………
2. I'm …………… years old.
3. I live in ……………
4. I come from ……………
5. There are …………… people in my family.
6. My favourite sport …………… because ……………
7. I like …………… music best because ……………
8. Last year I went to …………… on holiday. It was fun because ……………

2 Complete the sentences with *and*, *because* or *but*.
1. I like rock music …………… I don't like classical music.
2. My friends …………… I often go shopping together.
3. I never watch football …………… I don't like the sport.
4. My favourite meals are curry …………… pizza.
5. I don't play much sport …………… I don't have time.
6. I enjoy playing the guitar …………… I'm not very good!

3 Tick (✓) three sentences you could say if the examiner says, 'Tell me something about your best friend.'
1. I met my best friend at football club. ☐
2. It's good to have best friends. ☐
3. My brother's best friend's called Rob. ☐
4. My best friend lives in my street. ☐
5. My favourite TV show is about two best friends. ☐
6. I go to the same school as my best friend. ☐

4 Match the questions with the answers.
1. Who do you spend your free time with?
2. How often do you travel by train?
3. What's your house like?
4. What kind of sports do you enjoy?
5. When is your next holiday?
6. What did you last buy at the shops?

A. I like hockey and rugby.
B. Never. I always take the bus or drive to places.
C. I got a new winter coat. It's long and black.
D. My friends. I see my best friend every day after college.
E. It's nice. It's got six rooms and a garden.
F. In June. I'm going to Spain with some friends.

5 Complete the sentences with the prepositions *at*, *in*, *to* and *on*.
1. …………… my free time I like to draw. I'm not very good …………… drawing, but I enjoy it.
2. I don't have a lot of free time …………… the week, but I have more free time …………… the weekends.
3. …………… Saturdays, I go shopping with my friends and we usually go …………… a café for lunch.
4. I don't do very much …………… Sunday mornings. I sleep a lot and listen …………… music.
5. I usually have some free time …………… the evening. I enjoy talking …………… my friends on the phone.
6. I get home from college …………… six o'clock. Then I play …………… my computer before dinner.

SPEAKING BANK

Part 2 Phase 1

The examiner gives you and your partner some pictures to look at. The examiner asks you and your partner if you like or dislike the different activities, things or places shown in the pictures. You reply and give reasons for your opinions. You and your partner should talk together about the pictures.

Exam help

- Look at your partner when you speak to her/him.
- Look at each picture and say if you like or dislike what it shows.
- Give a reason for your opinion.
- Sometimes you can talk about a picture first and sometimes your partner can talk about a picture first.
- Talk for as long as you can. The examiner will tell you when to stop.
- Don't stop talking if you don't know a word. Try to use other words to say what you want, or move on to talk about something else.

Useful language

Saying you like something and giving a reason

I like quiz programmes. I think they're interesting.
I like them because I love answering the questions.
I always love going to the beach because I love the sea!
I really enjoy swimming in the sea. That's why I love the beach.

Saying you dislike something and giving a reason

In my opinion, the cinema is boring. That's why I don't like it.
I don't like it because, for me, the films are often too long.
I don't really enjoy restaurants. I prefer picnics outside.
I don't like sports programmes. I like playing sport, not watching it.

Part 2 Phase 2

The examiner asks you and your partner one or two questions on the same topic as Phase 1.

Exam help

- Always listen carefully when the examiner asks your partner a question first because the examiner will then ask you, 'And what about you?'
- If you forget the question, ask the examiner to say it again.
- Use the vocabulary and grammar that you have learnt.
- Listen carefully to the instructions.
- If you're not sure what to do, ask the examiner to say it again.
- Speak clearly so that both examiners can hear what you say.

Useful language

I prefer spend**ing** my free time with friends **because** it's more fun.
I'm not sure. I think I prefer holidays by the sea.
I'd like to go to Asia on holiday one day.
Yes, I like going to the cinema, **too**.
Well, I don't really know, perhaps art exhibitions?

Practice Part 2

1 Complete the sentences with these words and phrases.

> enjoy   for me   opinion   prefer
> really   think

1. I .... like team sports.
2. In my .... museums are really interesting.
3. I .... that restaurants are a good place to go with your family.
4. I don't really .... watching comedy programmes.
5. I don't enjoy going for long walks. I .... cycling.
6. I don't like the summer because, ..., the weather's too hot.

2 Match 1–6 with A–F.

1. My favourite activity is surfing because
2. I prefer watching sport to
3. I like going to restaurants best because
4. I enjoy painting and drawing.
5. I like rock music, but
6. I enjoy watching films with my family, but

A. I like all kinds of art.
B. I prefer going to the cinema with friends.
C. I love being in the sea.
D. I love food!
E. I don't enjoy listening to classical music.
F. playing sport.

3 Complete the sentences with reasons.

1. I really enjoy cycling because …
2. I love food – that's why …
3. I like going shopping because …
4. I don't enjoy drawing because …
5. I really like music – that's why …
6. I like spending time outside – that's why …

4 Answer the questions. Use these ideas, or your own ideas.

> love films   like playing sports
> enjoy learning about the past

1. Do you think visiting museums is interesting? Why?

   ....

2. Do you think going to the cinema is fun? Why?/Why not?

   ....

3. Do you think watching sport on TV is boring? Why?

   ....

5 Put the words in the correct order.

1. your question. / I'm / I / understand / sorry, / didn't

   ....

2. you / the question, / please? / Could / repeat

   ....

3. that / Could / say / again, / you / please?

   ....

4. I / the question. / didn't / hear / sorry, / I'm

   ....

5. not / I / sure / that word. / understand / I'm

   ....

6. mean? / What / that / does

   ....

SPEAKING BANK

WRITING BANK

Part 6 A short message

In Part 6, you have to write a short message. You read an email or information about a situation, including three prompts for information. You have to decide what information is needed and write an email or message of 25 words or more, including all three points.

> Your friend Lee was sick on Friday and now wants to know about the English class project. Write an **email** to Lee.
>
> In your email say:
> - **what** he has to write about
> - **how much** he has to write
> - **when** he needs to complete it by.
>
> Write **25 words** or more.

Example answer

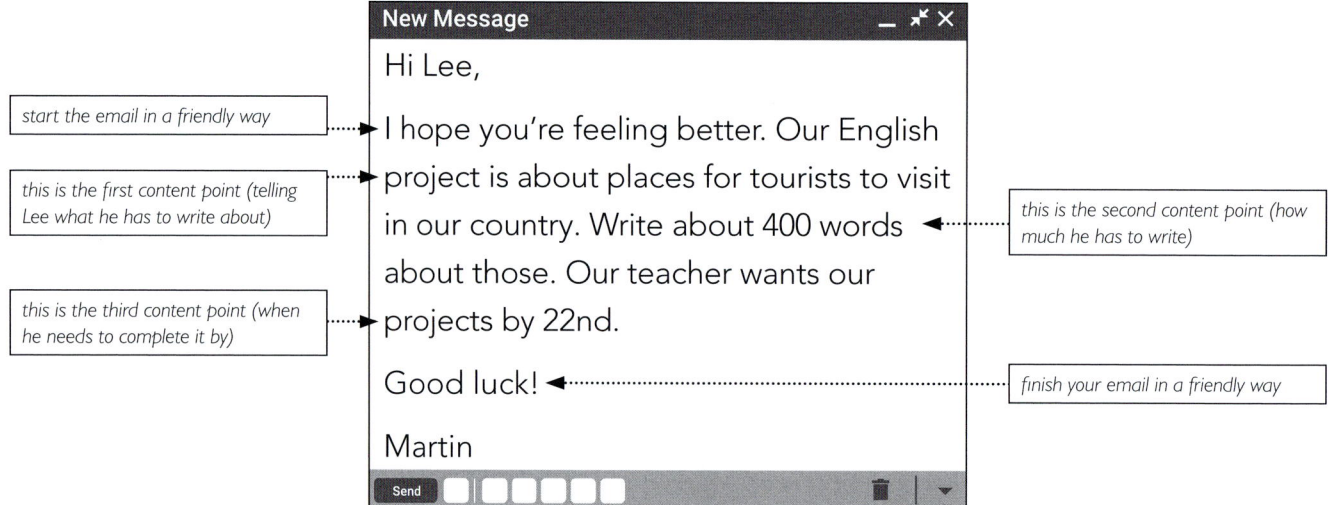

Exam help

- Read all the instructions carefully so that you understand the situation.
- Decide what kind of message you need to write and who it is for.
- Decide what kind of information you need to give.
- Remember to write in complete sentences and use the correct punctuation (capital letters, full stops, etc.).
- Use friendly language.
- Make sure that you include information for all three prompts.
- Start your email with a friendly greeting, for example, *Hi*.
- Finish your email in a friendly way.
- Check your email for grammar or spelling mistakes.
- Write at least 25 words.

Useful language

Starting an email
Hi,
Great news! I've got a new bike.
How are you?
Guess what? I'm going on a school trip to France!

Ending an email
Have a great weekend!
Please write to me soon.
See you next week!
Love

Practice Part 6

1 Complete the sentences with these prepositions.

| at | by | in | on | to | with |

1. The club starts .... 7.30 p.m.
2. We'll travel to the cinema .... train.
3. Do you want to play tennis .... Wednesday?
4. My birthday's .... June and I'm having a party.
5. I'm going .... the park. Would you like to come?
6. My dad's taking me to the football match. Do you want to come .... us?

2 Put the sentences in the correct order to make an email.

A You need to finish your essay before Friday.
B See you soon!
C You have to write 100 words.
D Kerry
E How are you?
F Hi Lee,
G You have to write an essay about your favourite film.

3 Correct the punctuation in this email.

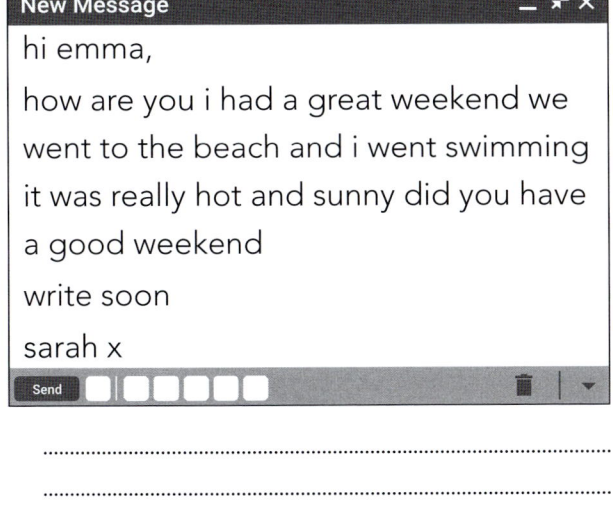

Planning your short message

- Read the question carefully so that you understand the situation. What are the three things you need to write about?
- Think of a friendly way to start your message, for example, *Hi David*, or *Dear Anna*,
- Think of a way to finish your message in a friendly way, for example, *See you soon!*, *Good luck!*

Checklist

When you finish writing a short message, use this checklist:

○ **Content**
Have you written about the three different pieces of information?
Have you written at least 25 words?

○ **Communicative achievement**
Is your short message friendly and easy to understand?

○ **Organisation**
Have you started and finished your short message in a friendly way?
Is all the information in a clear paragraph, or two short paragraphs?

○ **Language**
Have you used:
- complete sentences?
- some linking words?
- the correct grammar and tenses?
- some adjectives?
- correct punctuation?
- correct spelling?

Part 7 Story

In Part 7 you have to write a short story based on three pictures.

Look at the three pictures.
Write the story shown in the pictures.
Write **35 words** or more.

Example answer

Use different verb tenses to describe what happened.

*Use linking words such as **and** to join your ideas.*

Say how the person or people in the story are feeling.

> Two girls are riding their bikes beside a lake. It's a nice day. One girl is wearing sunglasses, and the other girl has a big hat. Then the girl's hat falls off – into the water! They stop their bikes and the girl picks up her hat. It's very wet. She's sad.

*Use time words like **then** to show what order things happened*

Use a variety of adjectives.

Exam help

- ✓ Describe each picture.
- ✓ Make sure that your story has a beginning, a middle and an end.
- ✓ Say who you can see in each picture and what the people are/were doing.
- ✓ Say where the story happened.
- ✓ Include words that explain when things happened (for example, *Later*).
- ✓ Include words like *because* and *so* if possible.
- ✓ Include some adjectives.
- ✓ Check your work for grammar or spelling mistakes.
- ✓ Write at least 35 words.

Useful language

In a story you need …

- verbs in the past tense (for example *was*, *ran*, *saw*, *opened*) because the story happened in the past.
- words that link the actions in the past (for example *after that*, *later*, *when*) to make your story easy to follow.
- a variety of adjectives and expressions (for example *terrible*, *afraid*, *surprised*, *suddenly*) to add interest to your story.

WRITING BANK

Practice Part 7

1 Choose the correct adjectives.

1. We laughed a lot because it was a very *fun / funny* story.
2. Kirsty thought the film was very *boring / bored*.
3. The party was *brilliant / terrible*! Everyone had a great time.
4. The concert was so *noisy / quiet*! I couldn't hear what my friends were saying.
5. My friend Oliver sang in front of the whole school. I think he's very *careful / brave*.
6. Everyone knew the actor. He was very *famous / favourite*.
7. Liam was *alone / worried* because he couldn't find his keys.
8. The man couldn't lift the box because it was very *heavy / hungry*.

2 Choose the correct form of the verbs in the story.

Joe **(1)** *gets / was getting* ready for school. He **(2)** *was having / had* one shoe but **(3)** *can't / couldn't* find his other shoe. He **(4)** *looked / 'll look* in the cupboard under the stairs. His shoe **(5)** *wasn't being / wasn't* there. Suddenly he **(6)** *is seeing / saw* it. His cat **(7)** *was sitting / sits* on it! Joe **(8)** *laughed / laughs*.

3 Complete the paragraph with these words and phrases.

| After   Later that day   That morning |
| Last Saturday morning   When |

(1) .... Oliver visited his aunty.
(2) ...., Oliver's aunty was feeling ill.
(3) .... his visit, Oliver decided to buy some flowers for her. **(4)** ...., he gave the flowers to his aunty. **(5)** .... she saw the flowers, she was very happy.

Planning your story

- Look at all three pictures and understand what the story is about.
- Decide where and when the story took place
- Think about how to describe each picture. Who can you see and what are the people doing?
- Think of some words that show when things happened, for example, *First, then, later, when, after that.*

Checklist

When you finish writing a story, use this checklist:

Content
Have you written about each of the three pictures?

Communicative achievement
Is your story clear and easy to understand?
Have you written at least 35 words?

Organisation
Does your story have a clear beginning, middle and end?

Language
Have you used:
- complete sentences?
- some linking words?
- the correct grammar and tenses?
- some adjectives?
- correct punctuation?
- correct spelling?

WRITING BANK

VISUALS FOR SPEAKING TESTS

TEST 1

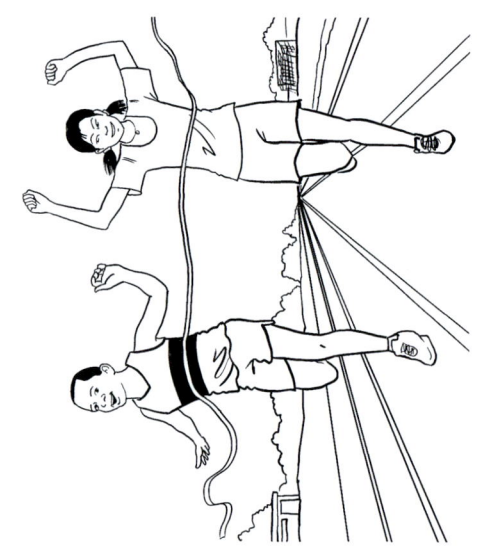

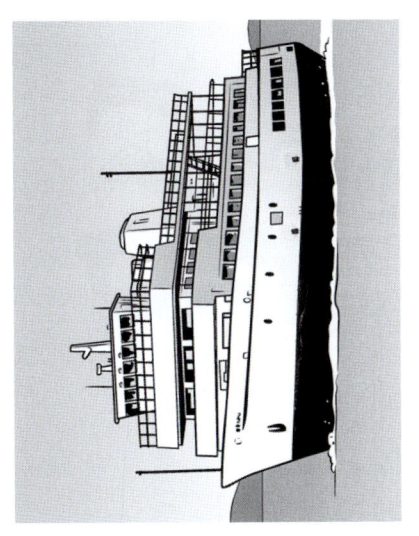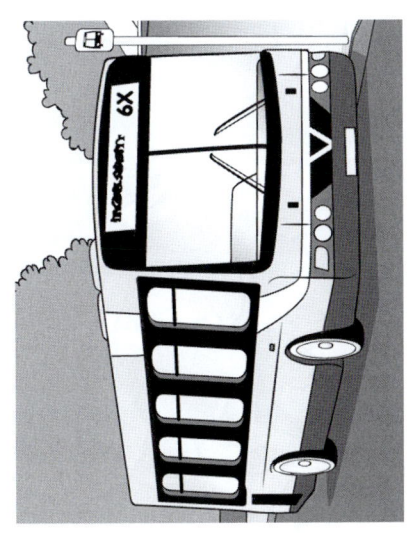

TEST 5

VISUALS FOR SPEAKING TESTS

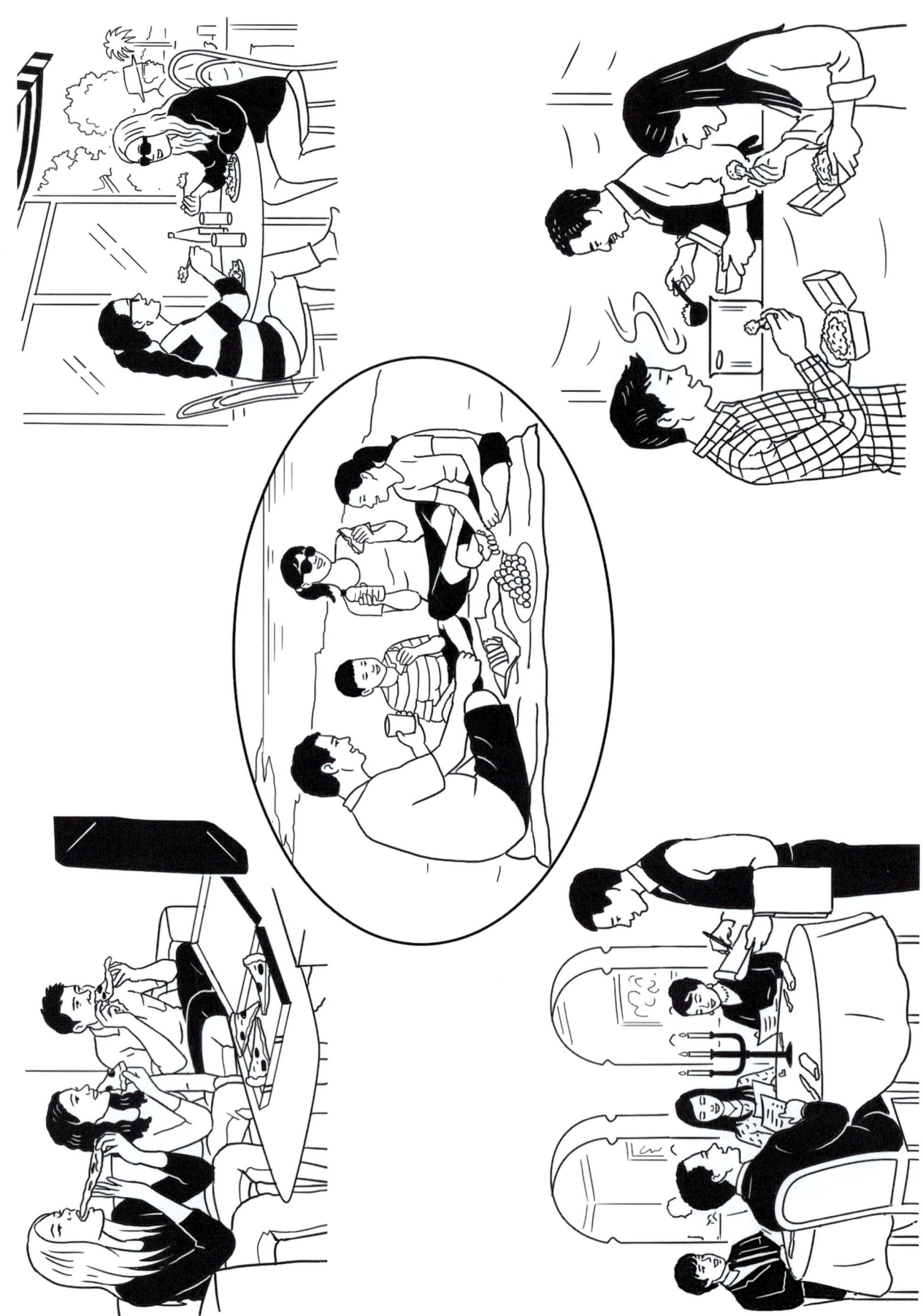

VISUALS FOR SPEAKING TESTS

KEY (ALSO FOR SCHOOLS) GENERAL QUESTIONS

1 **What is the format of the KEY and KEY for Schools exams, and are all the papers taken on the same day?**
➤ There are three papers:
Reading and Writing (1 hour) Listening (about 30 minutes) Speaking (9–10 minutes). Papers 1 and 2 are always taken on the same day. The Speaking Test may be taken on the same day or on a different day.

2 **How is the KEY for Schools exam different from the KEY exam?**
➤ KEY for Schools follows the same format as KEY. The difference is that the content and topics in KEY for Schools are more suitable for the interests and experiences of younger people.

3 **What level is the KEY exam?**
➤ The KEY exam is aligned to the Council of Europe Common European Framework for Reference (CEFR) and is level A2 in the CEFR.

4 **Are the KEY and KEY for Schools exams suitable for students from any culture?**
➤ Yes. All tasks are written to avoid any cultural bias.

5 **What are the grade ranges for the KEY and KEY for Schools exam?**
➤ There are four grades with fixed values: Pass with merit = 85–100%; Pass = 70–84%; A1 = 45–69%; Fail = 44% and below.

6 **Do I have to pass each paper in order to pass the exam?**
➤ No. Each paper doesn't have a pass or fail mark. The final mark a candidate gets is an average mark obtained by adding the marks for all three papers together.

7 **What mark do I need to get to pass the exam overall?**
➤ To achieve a pass in the KEY or KEY for Schools exam a candidate must receive a minimum of 70% as an overall average.

8 **When can I use pens or pencils in the exam?**
➤ In the exam a candidate must use pencil in all papers.

9 **If I write entirely in capital letters, does this affect my score?**
➤ No. Candidates are not penalised for writing in capitals in the exam.

10 **Am I allowed to use a dictionary?**
➤ No, you aren't.

11 **Is correct spelling important in Paper 1 (Reading and Writing)?**
➤ It is important only in Parts 5, 6 and 7.

12 **Is correct spelling important in Paper 2 (Listening)?**
➤ It is important only in Part 2.

13 **In Paper 1 (Reading and Writing) will extra time be given for me to transfer my answers to the answer sheet?**
➤ No. You must transfer them in the 1 hour you are given to complete the exam.

14 **In Paper 2 (Listening) will extra time be given for me to transfer my answers to the answer sheet?**
➤ Yes. You will be given some time at the end of the test for this.

15 **How many times will I hear each recording in Paper 2 (Listening)?**
➤ You will hear each recording twice.

16 **Can I ask any questions if I don't understand something in Papers 1 (Reading and Writing) and 2 (Listening)?**
➤ The only questions you can ask are those that relate to the rules of the exam. For example, the time you have, where to write your name or your answers, completing the answer sheet, whether or not you can use a pen, etc. You cannot ask for any help with the test items themselves.

17 **Can I ask any questions if I don't understand something in Paper 3 (Speaking)?**
➤ Yes. You can ask the examiner to repeat a question in Part 1 and to repeat the instructions in Part 2. If you still don't understand, tell the examiner you don't understand. You can ask your partner to repeat or clarify when they are asking you questions or answering your questions in Part 2.

18 **In Paper 3 (Speaking), do I have to go in with another student? Can I choose my partner?**
➤ You cannot be examined alone. You will usually be examined with one other candidate, but if you are one of the last candidates to be examined and there is an odd number of candidates on the day, you may be examined in a group of three. In some smaller centres you may be able to choose your partner, but in bigger centres this may not be possible.

19 **In Paper 3 (Speaking), is it a good idea for me to prepare what I am going to say in Part 1?**
➤ It is a good idea to practise saying your name, spelling your surname and talking about yourself (your family, school, school subjects, hobbies, etc.). It is important that you answer the examiner's questions and that you do so naturally, so listen carefully and think about the questions you have been asked. If you give a prepared speech you may not answer the examiner's question. You will lose marks if your answers are irrelevant.

20 **In Paper 3 (Speaking), what if I can't understand my partner in Part 2 or if he/she can't understand me?**
➤ If there is a communication breakdown between you and your partner in Part 2, try to solve the problem between you. For example, ask your partner for clarification or to repeat a question or an answer, or help your partner if necessary. You will be given credit for helping your partner if he/she is having difficulty.